WHOLE CHURCH

WHOLE
CHURCH

- -

LEADING FROM FRAGMENTATION TO ENGAGEMENT

Mel Lawrenz

A LEADERSHIP ❊ NETWORK PUBLICATION

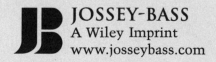

JOSSEY-BASS
A Wiley Imprint
www.josseybass.com

Published by Jossey-Bass
A Wiley Imprint
989 Market Street, San Francisco, CA 94103-1741—www.josseybass.com

Library of Congress Cataloging-in-Publication Data

Lawrenz, Mel.
  Whole church : leading from fragmentation to engagement / Mel Lawrenz   1st ed.
      p.   cm.
  Includes bibliographical references and index.
  ISBN 978-0-470-25934-4 (cloth)
      1. Christian leadership.   2. Church controversies.   3. Church–Unity.   I. Title.
  BV652.1.L32 2009
  253—dc22

                                                            2008055665

Printed in the United States of America
FIRST EDITION
HB Printing   10 9 8 7 6 5 4 3 2 1

LEADERSHIP NETWORK TITLES

The Blogging Church: Sharing the Story of Your Church Through Blogs, Brian Bailey and Terry Storch

Leading from the Second Chair: Serving Your Church, Fulfilling Your Role, and Realizing Your Dreams, Mike Bonem and Roger Patterson

The Way of Jesus: A Journey of Freedom for Pilgrims and Wanderers, Jonathan S. Campbell with Jennifer Campbell

Leading the Team-Based Church: How Pastors and Church Staffs Can Grow Together into a Powerful Fellowship of Leaders, George Cladis

Organic Church: Growing Faith Where Life Happens, Neil Cole

Off-Road Disciplines: Spiritual Adventures of Missional Leaders, Earl Creps

Reverse Mentoring: How Young Leaders Can Transform the Church and Why We Should Let Them, Earl Creps

Building a Healthy Multi-Ethnic Church: Mandate, Commitments, and Practices of a Diverse Congregation, Mark DeYmaz

Leading Congregational Change Workbook, James H. Furr, Mike Bonem, and Jim Herrington

The Tangible Kingdom: Creating Incarnational Community, Hugh Halter and Matt Smay

Leading Congregational Change: A Practical Guide for the Transformational Journey, Jim Herrington, Mike Bonem, and James H. Furr

The Leader's Journey: Accepting the Call to Personal and Congregational Transformation, Jim Herrington, Robert Creech, and Trisha Taylor

Whole Church: Leading from Fragmentation to Engagement, Mel Lawrenz

Culture Shift: Transforming Your Church from the Inside Out, Robert Lewis and Wayne Cordeiro, with Warren Bird

Church Unique: How Missional Leaders Cast Vision, Capture Culture, and Create Movement, Will Mancini

A New Kind of Christian: A Tale of Two Friends on a Spiritual Journey, Brian D. McLaren

The Story We Find Ourselves In: Further Adventures of a New Kind of Christian, Brian D. McLaren

Missional Renaissance: Changing the Scorecard for the Church, Reggie McNeal

Practicing Greatness: 7 Disciplines of Extraordinary Spiritual Leaders, Reggie McNeal

The Present Future: Six Tough Questions for the Church, Reggie McNeal

A Work of Heart: Understanding How God Shapes Spiritual Leaders, Reggie McNeal

The Millennium Matrix: Reclaiming the Past, Reframing the Future of the Church, M. Rex Miller

Shaped by God's Heart: The Passion and Practices of Missional Churches, Milfred Minatrea

The Missional Leader: Equipping Your Church to Reach a Changing World, Alan J. Roxburgh and Fred Romanuk

The Ascent of a Leader: How Ordinary Relationships Develop Extraordinary Character and Influence, Bill Thrall, Bruce McNicol, and Ken McElrath

Beyond Megachurch Myths: What We Can Learn from America's Largest Churches, Scott Thumma and Dave Travis

The Elephant in the Boardroom: Speaking the Unspoken About Pastoral Transitions, Carolyn Weese and J. Russell Crabtree

CONTENTS

PART THREE
THE DYNAMICS OF THE WHOLE CHURCH 103

ABOUT LEADERSHIP NETWORK

Since 1984, Leadership Network has fostered church innovation and growth by diligently pursuing its far-reaching mission statement: to identify, connect, and help high-capacity Christian leaders multiply their impact.

Although Leadership Network's techniques adapt and change as the church faces new opportunities and challenges, the organization's work follows a consistent and proven pattern: Leadership Network brings together entrepreneurial leaders who are focused on similar ministry initiatives. The ensuing collaboration—often across denominational lines—creates a strong base from which individual leaders can better analyze and refine their own strategies. Peer-to-peer interaction, dialogue, and sharing inevitably accelerate participants' innovation and ideas. Leadership Network further enhances this process through developing and distributing highly targeted ministry tools and resources, including audio and video programs, special reports, e-publications, and online downloads.

With Leadership Network's assistance, today's Christian leaders are energized, equipped, inspired, and better able to multiply their own dynamic Kingdom-building initiatives.

Launched in 1996 in conjunction with Jossey-Bass (a Wiley imprint), Leadership Network Publications present thoroughly researched and innovative concepts from leading thinkers, practitioners, and pioneering churches. The series collectively draws from a range of disciplines, with individual titles offering perspective on one or more of five primary areas:

1. Enabling effective leadership
2. Encouraging life-changing service
3. Building authentic community
4. Creating Kingdom-centered impact
5. Engaging cultural and demographic realities

For additional information on the mission or activities of Leadership Network, please contact:

Leadership Network
(800) 765-5323
client.care@leadnet.org

ACKNOWLEDGMENTS

Someone once asked a pastor how long it took him to prepare a sermon, and he wisely answered, "A lifetime." I cannot acknowledge everybody who has helped me learn to shepherd over the past four decades, but here are a few.

Pastor David Hughes and Pastor Bill Shepherd (what a great name for a pastor!) let me be their pastoral assistants over several summers when I was barely twenty years old, even allowing me to share in the preaching. They showed me the essence of shepherding: visiting the sick, supporting the grieving, being ready for the next opportunity and the next problem, leading in worship.

I am deeply grateful for the influence of Stuart Briscoe in my life ever since I was a college student. When I first heard him preach I discovered the explosive power of proclamation and the innate veracity of Scripture. He has modeled an integrity and focus of ministry that is compelling. I can only hope that those of us trained by him will be energized by the Word and the Spirit as he has, will not get bogged down in minor issues, and will keep as happy a spirit as his in the trenches of church ministry.

There are too many people to count at Elmbrook Church over the years who have shaped my values and perspectives of ministry. I am grateful for the dozens of pastors I've gotten to work with over the years, each one unique, each one trying in his or her way to lead people to a God-filled life. I am glad for colleagues who all share in the sense of our competence in Christ and our incompetence without Christ.

The members of the church teach me continually about what matters in ministry. Their encouragement has strengthened me so many times, and their longing for an ever deeper and wider impact has motivated me.

I am blessed to have a partner in ministry, my wife, Ingrid, who has always willingly accepted the cost of leadership, who challenges and supports me, who has incredible insight and wisdom, and who insists that the call of God be louder than any other voice.

And as for book writing—I am deeply grateful to work in partnership with the good people at Leadership Network whom I've gotten to know over the years, and for new friends at Jossey-Bass who are clearly focused on producing quality books to help leaders. Thank you, Sheryl Fullerton, for believing and reminding me that publishing is both important and fun at the same time.

PART ONE

WHOLE CHURCHES AND FRAGMENTED CHURCHES

1

FOSTERING WHOLE CHURCHES

THE BIG IDEA

The gospel we stand for is a message of wholeness (shalom, salvation, spiritual health) for broken people and a broken world, and that wholeness must be reflected in our churches. Powerful forces are constantly fragmenting us and our churches, but it is still possible to be a Whole Church. Engaging God's supply with human need is a call for the twenty-first-century church.

SICK OF FRAGMENTATION

I have never met a pastor or other church leader who said that he or she wanted to foster a partial or broken church. Churches are meant to be whole. And I have never met a leader who said he or she wanted to promote fragmentation in the church—although any of us can be blind to the forces of fragmentation, and in our worst moments we as church leaders may be the source of or promoters of fragmentation.

None of us wants to see the church we serve be satisfied with being incomplete, skewed, prejudiced, parochial, limited. We know that churches, human as they are, will be all these things, but we also know that our churches have a higher calling to draw from the fullness of Christ and demonstrate the fullness of Christ. This book is meant to be a gift of encouragement to church leaders who feel war-torn by the battles that arise from our own

3

foolishness in the church, and to church leaders who feel as if they have been on a search for the holy grail of church models, that the search hasn't been very fruitful, and that they can't exactly remember what they were searching for in the first place.

I am sick of fragmentation. How about you?

The one community that should understand wholeness—and explore it, embrace it, luxuriate in it, model it, enhance it, promote it—is the church. The one organization that can hold together despite having a head who is invisible and a mission that embraces all of life—is the church. The one collection of people who should experience the most joy, be committed to the most focused agenda, and have an ongoing sense of expectancy—is the church.

So why is it that our churches can be the most

fragmented,

restrictive,

tense,

controlling,

uptight,

mean-spirited,

small-minded,

self-righteous,

spirit-smothering,

organizations you can find . . . and what's more, believe that churches are really supposed to be battlegrounds, as if God intended things to be this way?

There is a better way.

It is time to rediscover the *Whole Church*. It is there for us, just an arm's length away. A Whole Church is a local congregation believing that it is called to the whole purpose of God in and through the church, rather than to some specialization. A Whole Church means leading people in practical ways into a true engagement with God (in worship and devotion), engagement with God's people (in true *koinonia*), engagement with the community (deployed witness), and engagement with the world (making real connections across national lines). And when we commit to all levels of engagement, we see a truly integrated picture of ministry and church life: worship leads to mission, community enhances personal devotion, witness leads us back to worship again. We see spiritual life with forward momentum as being the great cohesive dynamic of life. We see the gears of the church coming together, fully engaged, and then the engine of God's power moving the church forward.

Wholeness is our best defense against arbitrary personal ambition and against party spirit in a congregation. A vision of the Whole Church is the big idea that elevates us above our squabbles and our small-mindedness. In those seasons when a sense of Whole Church is the spirit of the majority of a congregation, we see celebration come naturally, and a congregation can come through even the kind of crises that are like earthquakes that shift the ground on which people stand.

Does this sound too idealistic? Are you saying to yourself, "Whoever this author is, he's not offering a very realistic picture of the church—not of my church, anyway." Well, I assure you that in almost three decades of being a pastor, I've seen every kind of disappointing behavior we all see in our churches. I cringe whenever I've been the root of a problem, and I live with the rueful memories of when I've spoken carelessly or led the church down a dead-end street. I cling to the biblical view of the church that is lofty in aspirations and measured in expectations. Wholeness is there for us, at arm's length, but our churches will always be susceptible to division and fragmentation. We hear the gears grind. We surge ahead, but we also get stuck. Leaders pull in different directions, following different agendas. New special interest groups may be born at any time in a congregation, and the old special interest groups hang on out of an instinct for self-preservation. We go to a leader conference and come back home thinking that we have to import somebody else's idea and change the whole course of the church one more time—and we hear our coworkers groan. You introduce change in the church, and you get e-mails right away accusing you of pulling the congregation apart rather than pulling it together. And, amazingly, the accusers believe they know exactly what your motives are. They have some telepathic capacity to read your mind and know that you are creating this trouble because you are self-centered and indifferent to the feelings of others. They always knew you intended to be unfaithful to God.

Pause. Groan. Catch your breath.

Whole Church is at the same time both an unattainable goal and also the only goal worth striving toward. It is about unity, but not the kind of unity that is grudging and obligatory. Certainly not unity for unity's sake—which never happens. On those days when we see the church we serve in come together, it is because a crisis or a challenge or an opportunity compels us to attach ourselves to God in that mysterious way that pulls us together. Unity isn't a slogan; it's becoming what we are in Christ.

And that is where leaders come in. Effective leaders do not sit back on their heels in status quo mode, and they do not charge ahead, way ahead, of the congregation until they are so isolated that they preach to the air. As someone once said, "If they ain't followin', you ain't leadin'."

Effective church leaders lead congregations into activities that provide a realistic sense of forward momentum, and they look for every cohesive experience available for the staff, for the congregation, and for themselves. (And the best ideas those leaders borrow from other churches are for creating those cohesive experiences.) In our better days as leaders, we believe we are looking at a body, not a herd of people we've corralled into a big room on Sunday morning. And the ministry activities in which we choose to invest our finite amount of energy and time lead others to experience the Whole Church.

In this book you will encounter the stories of dozens of real-life churches and leaders who have gone through our common experience of watching the church alternately fragmenting and pulling together. At the end of each chapter are specific practical things to do to promote cohesion in your church.

Before going any further, let me say something about you, the reader. I wrote this book in honor of and in support of the many pastors and other church leaders who want to clarify their ministry stance in a way that is faithful to God's call to practical fruitfulness in this new millennium. (Or forget the millennium—just to get through this week.) I have worked at different times as a pastoral assistant, a youth pastor, an associate pastor, and a senior pastor in rural churches and metro churches, in a large church and in one church that had a couple dozen pews and thirty or forty in attendance (on a good Sunday). I've worked in mainline denominational churches and nondenominational churches.

I'm thinking of those of you who are looking for ways of doing ministry that are fresh and new, but not faddish. Ministry whose roots are in the kingdom of God and not the kingdom of Wall Street and Madison Avenue.

If you find the paradigm and practicalities of engagement helpful, you may wish to invite the leaders with whom you work (key lay leaders, church staff, board members) to read this book with you and discuss it.[1] No church is helped by leaders pulling in different directions or fretting that they are directionless or chasing the latest fashion that will be here and gone within a decade or less.

This book includes 325 concrete ideas for creating cohesion in your church (25 at the end of each chapter). To promote the Whole Church, we need inspired imagination and concrete ideas. Fragmentation is happening all the time; healing is happening all the time. But we need to see every day as an opportunity to promote the Whole Church.

Do we have any option but to commit ourselves to fostering Whole Churches? Bringing together God's supply and human need at every level of engagement is the boldest, most strategic move we can make. It is the way God's Spirit works.

THE REAL STUFF

The visitation line snaked through the church lobby; hundreds of people, many sobbing at the placards displaying photos of Clint, inched their way forward before coming up to the grieving parents. The line continued down the church aisle to where the open casket was on display. By the time the funeral had started, two thousand people had gathered, many of them teenagers from different high schools around the city who knew Clint as that outstanding football player and just a really great guy. But this was not the first time that this had happened. Within that same year, two other teenagers from our church had also been killed in auto accidents, and then too, large crowds had gathered. Three times. It was beginning to seem bizarre. And in the three years prior we had seen a huge outpouring of the community and our church at the funeral of two church members, husband and wife, martyred in Uganda by nighttime raiders, and at the funeral of a nineteen-year-old girl who was shot and killed in the Humvee she was in on patrol in Baghdad. A beautiful young girl whose two sisters, one of them a twin, had been serving in Iraq at the same time. Three beautiful soldier sisters. Now two.

When I look out at crowds like that, at those hushed moments when our mouths are stopped and when the congregation consists of mature believers and complete nonbelievers and everything in between—I always think about how these are moments of engagement. We come face-to-face with that bold line between life and death. It is a moment of reckoning. But in this engagement with God, engagement of church members with each other, and engagement with the wider community—what do we do? What do we say? It is a time when church leaders know: this is why we are here. This is why God gave the church. This is the real stuff.

Occasionally I go to Bob and Win's house to have them pray for me. I feel greedy doing so, because I know that even without that request, Bob and Win pray for me every day. And I mean pray. They talk to God the Father and Jesus and the Holy Spirit; they pour out their hearts. That has to be one of the main reasons they are the compassionate, generous people they are. They look at other people, and they see, with a precise vision, their real need. And they see the grace of God all around. They are living the verse in Hebrews which says, "See to it that no one misses the grace of God and that no bitter root grows up to cause trouble and defile many" (12:15). Some people just have their eyes open. They're not full of false spirituality, and it's not that they are spinning life in a way that things come out kind of God-ish. They really do see the blessings and the protections of God, and that must be what allows them to look realistically at the wounds of everybody around them as well.

(And "see to it that no one misses the grace of God" is an excellent definition of church ministry, too. "Seeing to it" means that leaders are to be sentinels of God's grace, sounding off and pointing in the direction of God's grace wherever we see it. Isn't that why people show up at a church in the first place—because they are looking for some source of hope?)

I pull into the gravel driveway of Bob and Win's modest home in Menomonee Falls at the end of a cul-de-sac. The front door—faced with a wood hand carving that Bob did years ago—usually swings open before I have a chance to knock. I usually seem to be running late, but Bob and Win measure their time well and do not fuss when they've waited for someone else. I've never seen them try to squeeze more into a day or out of a day than what is sensible.

Just a few steps to the right on the hardwood floor brings us into the small living room, with a few select pictures on the wall and a couch, a couple of chairs, and a rocking chair. They insist that I sit in that comfortable chair, and after a few minutes of chatting we get down to business. But this prayer time is not business-like at all. They just ask me how they can pray, I give them the four or five top things uppermost on my mind, they talk between them about which of them will pray about which topics, and they pray. This is the real stuff.

I can't enter that room without thinking back to thirty-five years earlier when, as a college freshman, I sat on that hardwood floor at Bob and Win's youth Bible teaching called "Forever Family." I was then a brand-new believer, listening to Win teach about the festivals in Leviticus. Now, all these years later, I'm the senior pastor of the church they attend.

Seventy or so teenagers used to crowd into that small living room and spill into the dining area, everyone sitting on the hardwood floor because there was no other way to do it. When the first few people came on a given evening, they helped carry all the furniture from the living room out onto the front yard, because more people could get in if there was no furniture in the room. So in January, there sat the furniture on top of the crusty snow of midwinter Wisconsin. People matter more than couches.

A CALL TO ENGAGEMENT

December of 1999 was filled with anticipation. When the world crossed the line from one century to the next and one millennium to the next, people weren't sure whether to be excited or frightened or bored. On December 31, 1999, people held their breath to see if many of the world's computers would stop working at the stroke of midnight because their algorithms could not understand 01/01/2000—the famous Y2K scare. Some scenarios splashed in the media had airplanes falling from the sky, power grids going down, people's furnaces failing and people freezing. Stores had runs on generators, dry goods, and ammunition. (Some people thought you had to have your gun loaded in case your neighbors tried to break into your house and steal your food in the weeks following the supposed catastrophe—an odd twist, I thought at the time, on being salt and light in the community.) People called the office of our church asking (in all sincerity) if we were going to stockpile provisions in the basement of the church. Would I give a sermon on the topic of the coming disaster?

And all the while we fussed about Y2K in late 1999, and some people feared a phantom crisis, a handful of young men from the Middle East were plotting how they could fly jets into office towers and landmarks twenty-one months later.

This is one of the things that drives me in ministry: no one knows where evil is lurking beneath the surface of things. Faith-building is preparing people for *anything* that may come.

It struck me during that time that God was calling us to *engage*. You won't find that as a missional word in English translations of Scripture, but the idea is there throughout. What I mean by engagement is *bringing together God's supply and human need*. It means closing what I call the God gap. This definition is important throughout this book. Christian leaders have been using the word "engagement" for a few years, but it is usually limited and undefined. "Engaging the culture" has meant seeing the films and reading the books and listening to the music nonbelievers are shaped by—being conversant with it all. Responding. Challenging. Offering alternatives. It's a good idea. "Engaging with world need" has meant opening our eyes to AIDS and poverty and illiteracy. That's a fantastic idea.

But for all of this to get beyond fine rhetoric where "engagement" is locked up in magazine articles, it has to be the driving dynamic *at every level of spiritual life* in real churches. We have to truly bring together God's supply and human need. I started to speak to our church—just as one church, one group of people looking for next steps in the new millennium, about four kinds of engagement:

1. *Engaging with God* (the life of worship and personal devotion)
2. *Engaging with God's people* (real *koinonia* through small groups and other means)
3. *Engaging with your community* (imaginative ways to distribute Christian witness through involvement in social needs—witness that is decentralized, grass roots, salt and light)
4. *Engaging with the world* (developing an awareness of and involvement in global mission)

I started to ask the members of our congregation at least once a year whether they can say with honesty, "I am engaging with God; I am engaging with God's people; I am engaging with my community; I am engaging with the world." Most people know where they are engaged and where they are not (unless they barely have a relationship with God or have fallen off a spiritual cliff and don't know which end is up).

Just look up the multiple definitions of *engagement* in the English dictionary, and the applications for church ministry are obvious:

Engage \in-gāj

To become involved in or participate in

To pledge or to promise

To assume an obligation

To become meshed or interlocked

To be attracted to or engrossed with

To draw into

To reserve to use

Engagement is bringing together God's supply and human need. It is the "bringing together" that is the transformational process for individuals and for a local church because it is extraordinarily easy for us to *say we believe* in divine supply and human need, but then in our ministry to fail to bring together the supply and the need. Too often the church talks about God's great provisions (grace, salvation, mercy), but then those provisions are not applied in real and practical ways in people's lives. This has resulted in disengaged Christians and disengaged churches. A lot of talk, little action. Disengaged worship is just going through the motions; there is no God-encounter. Disengaged congregations are gatherings of people that could be engaged with each other in a revolutionary community, but that somehow never get past cake and coffee in fellowship halls. Disengaged "missions" initiatives are merely exercises in writing checks and mailing them overseas. Disengaged evangelism keeps the gospel bound up in catch phrases that are increasingly meaningless to the nonbelieving world. Disengagement keeps us talking a good line as the church with little or no long-lasting effectiveness. We preach to the choir. We feel self-satisfied. We affect no one.

Engagement is a call for the twenty-first-century church. Not because it's our newest invention in making today's churches run well, but because it is the ancient way, so often forgotten, neglected, and layered over with so many distracting ambitions. On the one hand, we see a world more connected than ever before through technological communication advances, but on the other, what we learn is how fractured and fragmented the world, our communities, our families, and we ourselves are.

This is the time to engage.

Church leaders have a most serious responsibility in helping people personally **engage with God**. That's what people need. That's what they want. That's what God has called us to do. A hundred years from now, nobody is going to care who had the biggest church or the most-quoted catchphrase. What will matter is whether we engaged with God. And then we have a responsibility to help fellow believers **engage with each other** in meaningful *koinonia*. A church can be and must be a movement of people coming together, living the shared life, finding grace in the other. But we must not stop with engagement between God's people. By leading people into **engagement with their communities**, we release them into the great mission. In the world, but not of the world. The community of Christ infiltrating the surrounding community. And we must not stop there, but lead people into **engagement with the world**. An ordinary believer living an ordinary life in a small town in the middle of Nebraska can be a "world Christian."

Joining a two-week mission team to do construction work in Costa Rica can open a believer to the horizon of God's great work in the world. But we don't need plane tickets to be world Christians. Our vision of the great mission is only as limited as our spiritual imaginations. When we tell the stories (and tell them well), our people will thank us for transporting them to a higher place where nations are not distinguished by crayon colors as they are on a map. People will thank us for giving them an authentic sense of purpose.

EXPONENTIAL EFFECT

As we look at these four different kinds of engagement in this book, one of the most important dynamics to understand (and the most exciting, I think) is the cumulative effect they have on each other. Who cares if we can take many of the functions of a local church and divide them into four tidy boxes: engagement with God, engagement with God's people, engagement with the community, and engagement with the world? We need something more than another rubric that gives us a list, a sermon series, and a table of contents for a book.

Engagement is a movement. It is divine power reshaping human experience. Bringing God's resources into contact with human need is one way of interpreting what the "work of the Spirit" means. And here is the best part: when we lead the ministry of a church as a whole, and when we bring these different kinds of engagement into contact with each other, they have an exponential effect. The energy of one kind of engagement combines with the energy of other engagements, and things really get out of control!

There are two kinds of growth: numeric and exponential. If you have a fire burning a couple of logs and you add one log every fifteen minutes, the fire will burn steadily (that's numeric growth). But if every fifteen minutes you add one log for every one in the fire, then in one hour you'll have sixteen logs on the fire and a release of energy that is stunning (that's exponential growth).

If a church tries to get one hundred more people involved in small groups each year, that's a good thing. But if the energy of small groups is brought into the worship of the church, and global engagement is featured through storytelling in the worship time, and personal devotional life (engagement with God) is directed to community engagement, then the energy of each of these dynamics builds on each other. In other words, the Whole Church that mixes and matches and blends engagement with God, with God's people, with the community, and with the world will build a fire that feeds itself. A fire is never sustained when the logs fueling it are spread out and separated from each other. But that is our instinct in church leadership: to put spiritual life into categories and its own special rooms in the church.

LIFE IN THE CLUTCH

Engagement is like getting a car with a stick shift in gear.

A couple of years back, my son got his first car. He followed my suggestion in getting one with a standard transmission. It wasn't hard to convince him. An eighteen-year-old boy wants an engine he can rev and to lay down some rubber (unintentionally, of course). The day came when we picked up the car, and I gave him his first lesson in how to drive a stick shift. I knew what I was in for—the same embarrassing experience everyone has when learning how to put a car in gear manually, pressing the accelerator and easing up on the clutch. We went to a far corner of a large parking lot where there were no objects he could collide with and where no onlookers could watch the spectacle. He took occupancy of the driver's seat for the first time in this car, grinning from ear to ear. But it took at least a half-dozen attempts before he got the thing moving. Either he revved the engine far too much, the sound of it elevating to a high-pitched whirr that would make any neighborhood dog cock his head, or he didn't apply enough accelerator so, that when he let out the clutch, he killed the engine. When, after a few restarts, he did actually get the car moving, it lurched forward in spurts, the engine belching with each lunge. Our heads were alternately thrown forward and back (and I have to admit that I exaggerated these movements, just to keep him humble). At first he laughed. But after the sixth or seventh time, he wasn't laughing anymore. He became very intense, and I knew I had better not say much. And on days two and three, when he was still starting out by either killing the engine or catapulting himself down the street, he was sufficiently humbled to know that when you have power in your hands, you have to know how to use it. Starting the engine and idling it are easy—engagement is challenging.

When you are using a manual transmission, you are engaging the power of an engine with the dead-weight inertia of the automobile. The clutch is where power contacts need. And when power comes together with need, amazing things can happen. Now, if you'll forgive the limitations of a physical analogy, just consider this. Doesn't the church sometimes rev its engine up to incredible RPMs and remain motionless? Other times, lunge ahead and kill the engine? Still other times, engage the clutch, but with spurts and starts? But in those ministry moments when we get it right, when the gears come together and all the moving parts are engaged, transferring power to mass, we take off down the road and out onto the open highway. That's when we know: this is the way things are supposed to be.

We all learn the hard way that we can't rev the engine, talking about the theory of the power and the love of God, yet remaining disengaged. We just sound and look foolish. We also learn the hard way that to try new ideas or to impose somebody else's ideas on our congregations in ways that are artificial or rushed or full of hubris will only kill the engine.

Engagement is an easy word to say, but a challenge to make real.

Engagement is a way of life—for the believer and for churches. It is more than a program or task or project. It is social action and global involvement, but not merely so. Effective engagement with the needs of the world only begins as people are engaged with God.

- -

IN PRACTICE—COHESIVE IDEAS
FOR A WHOLE CHURCH

- -

1. Think of a time when your church was as unified as you have ever seen it. Make a list of the factors of unity and cohesion at work at that time.
2. Think of the last several times someone told you that your church was his or her place of hope and connection. What was happening in that person's life that made that possible?

3. Never reward the behaviors of people whose attitude is divisive.
4. Have a cup of coffee with another leader in the church who tends to pull in a different direction from you. Insofar as possible, make a personal connection.
5. Think of some way in which you can "see to it that no one misses the grace of God," by telling a story of grace sometime in the next week.
6. Discuss with two or three longtime, very mature members of the church what the long-standing history of the church is. Where are there deep-running fractures? Where is there unity?
7. Give up any desire to please everybody. Recommit to the role of the shepherd (who feeds, protects, and leads).
8. Apologize to someone you hurt in some way that created a fracture.
9. Be thinking of five key leaders in your church with whom you could discuss this book.
10. Develop confidential friendships with leaders from other churches who can be a sounding board for you.
11. Visit three other churches in the next year, not simply to copy ideas but to gain a wider and wider vision of the Whole Church.
12. Read three books this year that show the Whole Church in action (not theoretical books).
13. Step away from your church, take a real vacation, and then reset your vision of what is most important.
14. Find five things your church should stop doing because they are ineffective, drain energy and resources, and probably take away from the church more than they give.
15. Adopt a mind-set of continual incremental change. Always use the word "change" with a positive connotation when addressing the church. Use the word frequently.
16. Find a mature person or couple in your church who would consider it an honor to meet with you and pray for you.
17. Talk with your family members about whether you bring frustration from ministry work into your family, and decide together on what standards you will hold.

18. Ask *yourself* these four questions for right now: How am I (1) engaged with God, (2) engaged with God's people, (3) engaged with my community, and (4) engaged with the world?

19. Get a notebook and, as you go through this book chapter by chapter, allow yourself enough time to write out specific ideas that apply to your ministry.

20. Go further by checking out the additional resources at www.wholechurch.org.

21. Take a prayer and meditation day to give yourself some time to assess your personal ministry right now.

22. Confess to God the ways in which you have been the cause of fragmentation in someone else's life.

23. Read the seven letters to the churches in Revelation 2 and 3 and make notes on what the essential qualities of faithful churches are.

24. Decide that you as a leader will be bold in simplifying and focusing your ministry. Make a list of six ways in which you can do that in the next six months.

25. Go to the place where your church meets at a time when no one else is around. Have an hour of prayer, asking God to give you a vision of a Whole Church.

2

CONFLICT AND FRAGMENTATION

THE BIG IDEA
While we try to foster the Whole Church, we need to be aware of the dynamics of fragmentation that always exist in every church. The reality is that we will always face fragmentation because it arises directly out of human nature.

Conflict is the wart on the nose of the bride of Christ. The church wants to pretend that it is not there, but everybody can't help staring at it. Churches, after all, are supposed to be models of redemption, reconciliation, holiness, integrity. The bride is supposed to be beautiful. But the reason the church is called the bride of Christ is not because it is beautiful, but because it is loved. Here is a biblical truth we all must cling to: the holiness of the church does not derive from the holiness of its members, but from the holiness of its God and the holiness of the calling it has received from God. And because we are called to the high purposes of God for the Whole Church, on our better days we behave in a manner becoming of holiness.

THE REALITY OF FRAGMENTATION AND CONFLICT

The statistics in this chapter come from the Hartford Institute for Religion Research, which conducts extensive national surveys of churches of all different denominations.[1] (Also, where indicated, we reference a survey conducted by Christianity Today on church conflict.[2])

Fact: 75 percent of all church congregations report having experienced some level of conflict in the church in the past five years.

Fact: Although congregations view conflict as inevitable, one in four reported conflict serious enough to have a lasting impact on congregational life.

Fact: When asked what they believed the sources of conflict were, survey participants reported the following:

Source of Conflict	Percentage of Respondents
Church members' behavior	44
Money	42
Worship	41
Leadership style	40
Decision making	39
Program priorities	30
Theology	26

Fact: When pastors were surveyed (in the Christianity Today survey), they had a different perspective:

Source of Conflict	Percentage of Respondents
Control issues	85
Vision or direction	64
Leadership changes	43
Pastor's style	39
Financial	33
Theological or doctrinal	23
Cultural or social differences	22
Other	16

THE IMPACT OF CONFLICT

Respondents in the Hartford study reported the following impacts of conflict:

Impact of Conflict	Percentage of Respondents
Some members left the church	69
Reduced giving	39
Leader left the church	25

The Christianity Today survey asked pastors about the negative outcomes of church conflict; the following were their responses:

Negative Outcome of Church Conflict	Percentage of Respondents
Damaged relationships	68
Sadness	58
Decline in attendance	32
Leaders leave church	32
Loss of trust	31
Bitterness	29
Loss of communication with the congregation	3

Conflict is costly. So the obvious solution is to decide not to have conflict in the church, right?

Congregations are smarter than that, and church leaders should be too. Conflict is inevitable as long as we are human. The questions become how to lessen the frequency of conflict and how to deal constructively with conflict when it does arise. Keeping conflict contained is also important. Conflict between leaders is not the same thing as conflict in the congregation.

To use an analogy, husbands and wives who get into spats are unwise when they allow the conflict to spread to the children. The central parties involved in a conflict are the ones responsible for dealing with it. (And, speaking of marriage, when I have done premarital counseling and asked couples what they have learned as they have worked through conflicts, the couples that really worry me are those who say they've never had a conflict.)

All churches will have people leave. Some leave because they move; some because they believe another congregation will be a better place for their spiritual growth; others leave because they have been hurt or are angry; still others are acting spoiled and leave because they didn't get their way on something. These are vastly different motivations, and we do people a disservice unless we respond to them according to their specific motives. It will do no good, for instance, for a pastor to take it as a personal insult every time someone leaves. And it will not do for a congregation to consider it a crisis if anybody leaves. If someone leaves the faith, that is a spiritual crisis. If someone switches the congregation he or she attends, it is not a net loss for *the* Church.

USING CONFLICT CONSTRUCTIVELY

Most leaders and most congregations are smart enough not to view conflict as fatal. Congregations want their leaders to work out problems. We ask people not to give up on their marriages and to avoid divorce, and they expect leaders to try to work out difficulties in the church without quickly resorting to the severing of relationships. They look to leaders and say, We know you have the ability to use conflict as a growth opportunity, and we expect you to do so.

The Christianity Today survey of pastors indicated that on the other side of conflict, when the dust has settled, pastors can see many positive outcomes:

Positive Outcome of Conflict	Percentage of Respondents
Pastor became wiser	72
Conflict was a purifying process	44
Church gained a more defined vision	42
Improved communication with the congregation	35
Strengthened relationships	30
Reconciliation	16
Growth in church attendance	15

In the same survey, pastors were asked what their feelings were about the outcomes of the conflict:

Pastor's Feelings About the Outcomes of the Conflict	Percentage of Respondents
Felt stronger	60
Felt more hopeful	35
Was thankful	32
Felt broken	26
Was confused	16
Felt that the conflict was not over	9

Fact: Almost all the pastors (94 percent) reported positive results from the conflict they experienced.

DIAGNOSING FRAGMENTATION

Conflict may fragment a church, but a church can be fragmented even without conflict (and then the fragmentation itself, rather than specific problems, becomes the seedbed of conflict). The classic form of fragmentation is party spirit—and it is a scourge of the church today because we have a consumer mentality more than ever before. Party spirit has always been there. Just read 1 Corinthians 1:12: "One person says: 'I follow Paul'; another, 'I follow Apollos'; another, 'I follow Cephas'; still another, 'I follow Christ.'" Sound familiar? I like this preacher; I like that preacher; I like the last youth minister better; I want things to be the way they were twenty years ago; I want things to be just like that church across town.

If your church has a broad enough vision to value the Whole Church, then you will invite in and attract people from a diversity of economic, social, ethnic, racial, political, theological, and spiritual backgrounds. If your church is centered on the core essentials of the gospel, and if you avoid hobby horses and fads and social limitations, then you will have people responding to the deeply satisfying heart of the gospel—they will not have gathered at their particular church because of a particular bent. But here is the irony: the more diversity you have in a church, the greater the possibility for factions and party spirit.

But to add irony on top of irony, it is those churches that are much more restrictive, defined, and limited that tend to be susceptible to party spirit. Here is the dynamic: these churches are often organized on the principle of what they agree they are against, more so than what they are *for*. If the organizing principle is wall building, then wall building on the interior is often the consequence.

One little verse in Philippians that has always stuck in my head (why, I am not exactly sure) is "I plead with Euodia and I plead with Syntyche to agree with each other in the Lord" (4:2). Now we don't know who these two women were. Their names mean nothing to us (for parents looking for a biblical name for a baby, Euodia and Syntyche appear to be wide open). Nevertheless, there was some conflict between these two, something that warranted an apostle's including a charge for unity in an epistle. But it isn't

"Can't we all just get along?" but rather "agree with each other *in the Lord.*"

I go to a sports arena to watch a contest, which is regulated conflict, and it's entertaining. There is nothing entertaining about conflict in a church (and God help us if we ever are titillated by a ruckus that's making the dust fly in some corner of the church—or if we take any satisfaction from seeing the commotion of a fracas in the church up the road). Agreeing "in the Lord" is an invitation to turn the arena into an amphitheater where a solitary voice arrests our attention.

VALUES: SAVING US FROM OURSELVES

I'd like to put an exclamation point at the end of each sentence in this section, but I'll just do it once.

Values save us from ourselves!

Whether the values are stated or not, every church has a value system, and when the values are truly inspired by God, they are our best hope of rising above conflict and fragmentation and of being drawn together as a Whole Church. Every church should be able to say why it does what it does. Values are the why behind the why. Values are a judgment of what is important, what is essential, what is nonnegotiable. Values are a way of saying, This is good and this is right. Values organize our experiences under our principles; they precede our action plans. Values are our moral and ethical center. They reflect what we cherish and treasure—even what we will die for.

A church can have rotten values, and usually in that case the values go unstated. If what is most important is "We want to be comfortable," "We want to have a respectable image," "We want to keep undesirables out," or "We want to be better than the church up the road," then that church might as well not call itself a church, because it has little to do with the intent of Jesus.

We must reinforce the foundational power of values: they are the why behind the why. Why are we open to outsiders? Because that's the heart of Jesus. Why do we want to grow in outreach and depth? Because Jesus wants as many people rescued as possible. Why do we want multiple generations in our church? Because we are Christ's body, and the members of the body need each other.

Values are what the newcomer senses when he or she shows up. Values are what shape our strategic decisions—and all the small decisions we make every day. When we decide to add or subtract a staff member, that decision should be based on what is truly important—what we value.

Almost any church will benefit from a thoughtful discussion of what its values are. Years ago, the following was the definition derived in our church, but we also reexamine and revise it occasionally:

Centrality of the Word

Evangelical witness

Unity in diversity

Priesthood of all believers

Welcoming environment

Freedom to fail

Commitment to growth

Good values save us from ourselves because they elevate us above the fights and squabbles of conflict. Good values prevent us from being satisfied with fragmentation. What makes a Whole Church possible is not just what we do (tactics) or the reason why we do what we do (strategy), but the why behind the why: a commitment to the things that matter to Christ (values).

IN PRACTICE—COHESIVE IDEAS FOR A WHOLE CHURCH

1. Find a good time to have a discussion with your staff about conflict in the church. Use this chapter, other parts of this book, or other reading as the substance of the discussion.
2. Have that discussion and others like it when there is no major conflict in the church, so that the discussion is not limited by people's personal feelings, but rather is guided by a more principled approach.

3. Take a half day to contemplate and pray about the overt and covert conflicts you are in right now.

4. If the people who know you best tell you that you are overcontrolling, take it seriously and let other people help you get to a better state of faith. Overcontrolling behavior leads to continual conflict.

5. Ask God to help you be free from anxiety about a conflict over which you have no further control.

6. When someone comes to you with a "sky-is-falling" attitude because of a conflict, help that person understand that conflict is part of life and that there are almost always steps to be taken toward resolution.

7. Spend some time reflecting on conflict resolutions that you witnessed years ago.

8. As a leader, surround yourself with other mature people who are not contentious by nature and who place a high value on peace.

9. When recruiting for leadership, look for people who have demonstrated skills in conflict management (at a personal level).

10. Head off conflicts as early as possible; don't let them fester.

11. Discern when avoidance of conflict is the best route.

12. Think of one situation that you know has needed to be confronted for a long time, and take the next step (test anything new you may have learned from this reading).

13. Remember this sage advice: "least said, soonest mended." Think of one situation where it really is best if you keep your mouth shut.

14. If there is someone who is continually a source of conflict, join with one or two other leaders and figure out how to calmly address the destructive pattern.

15. Be prepared, in the worst of circumstances, and having exhausted all other efforts, to tell a truly divisive person that his or her ongoing relationship with the church is threatened unless his or her pattern changes (Titus 3:10).

16. Watch out for bringing conflict in the church into your home and family. If there is reason to believe that you are taking

your frustrations out on your family, admit that to your family and come up with strategies to avoid this fatal pattern.

17. Call church members to rise above preference and party spirit, which are major weaknesses in a consumer society. Do not shape the church's program strictly according to preference.

18. Unleash the unifying power of the Word of God in preaching and teaching. Be enthusiastic about the discovery of substantive scriptural truth, and let the boldness of that truth bring people together.

19. Make the good news of Jesus Christ the core unifying principle in your church—in reality, not just rhetoric.

20. Lead your congregation into a culture of service (Phil. 2). Idleness leads to crankiness. Work leads to joy.

21. Develop a way for the leaders of your church to have a probing investigation of the values that underlie your church; plan a way for leaders to map out chosen values and determine how those values will shape your ministry in the next year.

22. Make managing conflict in your family your highest priority.

23. Develop a lifestyle of work and rest that keeps you fresh. Tired and worn-down people produce conflict, usually unintentionally.

24. Suggest that your church board have a substantive discussion about conflict and its management.

25. Be ready for the next conflict. It is only as far away as the next group of people. But don't let conflict steal your joy in Christ.

3

GETTING THE WHOLE CHURCH ENGAGED

THE BIG IDEA
Our only hope against the forces of fragmentation is a
steady, cohesive movement in the lives of believers and in
the life of a church. This happens when God's supply is
brought together with human need, when engagement
happens at four levels: (1) engaging with God, (2) engaging
with God's people, (3) engaging with your community, and
(4) engaging with the world.

ENGAGING WITH GOD

When I think about "engaging with God," Win and Bob always
come to mind. They begin their day talking to God, they take
phone calls and see people during the day and pray for them, and
they end their day in prayer. They remind me that "practicing the
presence of God" is not difficult. But their engagement with God
doesn't stay stuck in impressive personal spirituality. At the other
end of the engagement spectrum, they are as engaged as anyone
I know in the global mission of the church. They intimately know
the needs of dozens of missionaries serving overseas. For a few
years, they served with a mission in Eastern Europe as spiritual
supporters, and, despite the fact that for now they live back in
Wisconsin and do little traveling, they remain fully engaged with
the world. The praying by which they personally engage with God
also brings them ready engagement with the world as they pray

intelligently and concretely and passionately about workers all over the world.

Getting people personally engaged with God is where the mission of the church begins. Any other mission we take up is puny and pitiful unless we take God with us into it. (And, of course, the reality is that God carries us into the mission.) This is where the ministry of the church begins. What am I doing as a pastor if I am not, through preaching and prayer, conversation and confrontation, helping people find ways to close the gap between themselves and God? If my efforts don't help people draw closer to God, I'd be doing more good if I were a plumber.

Engagement with God doesn't happen for anybody in a single moment. Even for those who have a Saul of Tarsus, Damascus Road, knocked-to-the-ground, struck-blind, shouted-at-by-Jesus experience, that is just the beginning of a lifetime of engagement with God. Jesus did say at one moment "it is finished" and then the gap was closed, the curtain of the temple torn in two, humanity reconciled to God. The Door had come, the Way had opened up, the peace had been established. And on that basis all of us who have announced the good news of Jesus—everywhere and in all generations—have been able to tell people that whatever their failures and faults, God has performed a decisive act that makes full redemption possible.

Engaging with God includes providing patterns of worship and personal devotion that on a daily and weekly basis close the gap. It also includes creating occasional spiritual growth initiatives for a congregation, and responding to crises—such as heart-rending funerals—in ways that bring God's supply in contact with human need when that need is most severe.

ENGAGING WITH GOD'S PEOPLE

The second kind of engagement we are called to foster as leaders in the church is that between God's people. That's what the church is, right? The body of Christ. The communion of saints. The temple of God built with all those living stones.

So why is it that sometimes people walk out of church feeling more lonely than when they walked in? Why does the church sometimes resemble the obligatory family holiday gathering where brothers and sisters continue years of giving each other the cold shoulder, someone demands to be the center of attention as always, teenagers escape as quickly as they can, and the taste of the food is the most pleasant thing?

All of us in church leadership know that community is a make-or-break issue. The church as community is not a recently discovered phenomenon, and it isn't even something we do—it is what we always were supposed to be.

One of the best ways (but not the only way) to lead people into effective engagement with each other in the church is through the ministry of small groups. I've belonged to three different groups since I became a believer, each one lasting for years. I remember the day Stuart Briscoe committed Elmbrook Church to meet in homes on a weekly basis so as to be more connected in the body of Christ than we were when gathered as a whole congregation. It was 1975, well before the new small group movement began. I was in college at the time. The call to gather in home cells seemed so right. So I went weekly to the home of Ruth and Mel, and the thought barely crossed my mind that I was the only college-age person there.

ENGAGING WITH YOUR COMMUNITY

Once when I was talking to our congregation about community engagement in a sermon, I had a salt shaker on the platform, and as I explained Jesus' salt metaphor for witness, I shook the salt liberally onto the platform from one side to the next. I noticed that this got people's attention. I know there was at least one custodian sitting out there thinking, Now *what's he doing, and how are we going to get this cleaned up between services?*

I think about Jesus' salt analogy all the time. If I go into any store, restaurant, gym, office, or medical facility in our community, I know that it is very likely I'll run into people from our church. If I don't recognize them, they'll recognize me. I was in a restaurant once when the waitress informed me that someone at another table had picked up my check—a nice little surprise. And as I left the restaurant, I scanned the tables to see if there was someone I knew to greet or smile at. Problem was, I saw four different tables where folks from our church were seated. So I smiled at them all, not daring to thank any of them for paying for my lunch, and not knowing at the time that it wasn't any of them, but someone else I didn't recognize.

These experiences always remind me that we really are salt. We are distributed. We are "out there." We are plants in the wild field of the world. We are road signs in a wilderness. The question is whether we will live up to this high calling. Will we show people the ways to bring God's supply together with human need, or will we characterize ourselves and our people as outcasts in a hostile world whose only security is to be found when we are clustered and cloistered with other believers?

Community engagement is not limited to special events where we get a few hundred people out to rake leaves or to paint buildings. Far too often, we wait around for someone to come up with a campaign or program, not realizing that we are already out of the salt shaker and that witness begins today, not tomorrow. You can even say, unless you're living as a recluse in your home, that your witness *is* happening whether you choose for it to happen or not. People are watching, they are reading you like a book, and they are drawing conclusions when they hear that you are one of those "believers."

I find that it is still a challenge to get our staff and leaders and congregation to think in immediate and decentralized terms on this issue. We tend to think of top-down, programmatic, central control. Perhaps it comes from our assumption that leaders must always be in the mode of planning, managing, and measuring the work of the church. We leaders tend to think of ourselves as generals directing the troops in the field, keeping things in order through a proper chain of command. But is that what God started at Pentecost, when he poured out his Spirit on thousands of people from all over the world, who apparently went home and began the work of witness? Who was it in headquarters in Jerusalem who gave step-by-step directives to the Jesus followers who were out at the edges of North Africa or Germania? Certainly church leadership means "directing the affairs of the church," as Paul wrote to Timothy. But if we as leaders limit people's actions to the confines of *our* vision as leaders, we disregard and undermine the Spirit-inspired imaginations of a vast network of witnesses who are already out there, just one step away from engaging in their communities. Vision is not limited to leaders. A good leader casts a wide eye to a sweeping horizon and then tells other people about what he or she sees (a vision), but is never surprised when someone else sees something more, or different. Many people get a turn in the crow's nest.

People need the light bulb of community engagement to come on in their heads by way of leadership through example, which in turn fires their imagination. Don't wait for that campaign that will get everyone in the church (and perhaps other churches) involved in a community-transforming moment. Communities are not changed by events. The wonder of salt is that it permeates.

Years ago, an associate pastor on our staff who was responsible for community engagement (at that time we called it urban ministry) was under a lot of pressure to come up with a big splashy master plan that would begin to transform the metropolitan area. That just wasn't his way of doing things, and those of us to whom he reported agreed with his instincts to be skeptical of the witness-in-a-box approach. We've had our experiences in our city when someone thought that this one project or campaign would be *the* catalyst we were all looking for to initiate a wave of spiritual renewal and revival. I've heard from lots of people over the years about how doing A-B-C would bring about revival. But although I respect and am inspired by the longing of these folks to see God break in to our metro area in a dramatic way, I've seen blanket initiatives come and go. Meanwhile, the salt is already sprinkled, and our communities are waiting to get a taste.

One day I asked this associate pastor to write up a list of what was actually happening in ministry to the wider metro area, connecting social need and Christian conscience and witness. And I remember being surprised at the list he showed me of dozens of authentic initiatives that were happening at a grassroots level. But they went unnoticed. People felt as if nobody was doing anything, but that was just ignorance. That's the thing about the grass roots. When you're looking high and expecting a redwood forest, you can miss what God is doing at the roots. What God is *choosing* to do at the roots.

We will always believe that we must do more and that we are only scratching the surface. Because we *are* only scratching the surface. There has never been a Christian community in any nation or empire in any century that could properly say, job done, society transformed, well done; pat ourselves on the back, put it in a book. The worldwide enthusiasm and confidence in the year 1900 (relative global stability, worldwide mission, invention and prosperity) led some Christians to a postmillennial assumption that Christ's kingdom really was fully dawning. But World War I and the Great Depression and World War II woke up the church to the reality that "Mission Accomplished" is never going to be appropriately voiced by the church in this age.

In later chapters we'll consider how to inspire a congregation to community engagement by inspiring people's imaginations.

ENGAGING WITH THE WORLD

The fourth and last engagement theme brings us to the question of how churches can connect with the global Christian movement. This is within the reach of any church of any denomination of any size. Put it however you like: the world is getting smaller all the time; the world is flat; globalization is the way the world works now. It's true. I first flew in a jet when I was in college. By the time my kids got to college, they were racking up miles on their frequent flyer accounts. Friends of our church listen in real time to the Sunday worship service via live Internet streaming. I get home at lunchtime on Sunday and have on numerous occasions received an e-mail from a friend who listened to the worship service in real time in Tokyo (10 PM local time) or who listened off a laptop in Indonesia, Spain, Tanzania, or a barracks in Baghdad.

But airplanes and the Internet are just tools. The real issue of engaging with the world has to do with how our churches are connected, heart and soul, with what is happening around the globe.

I remember Mark Rich as a custodian on our staff almost twenty years ago now. He was healthy and robust, and had the greatest smile. He was eagerly waiting for the day when he and his wife, Tanya, would be able to go to Panama as missionaries, not knowing that just months into their stay in Pucuro, he and two other men would be kidnapped from the compound and taken deep into Colombia, then held as hostages for years.

My two kids were just six and seven years old at the time. Our church prayed frequently for Mark and the other hostages. Kids seemed particularly compelled to pray for them. Around our dinner table it was virtually an everyday prayer voiced by any of us who prayed—not for two years or four years, but for eight years. It was as if Mark were part of our family, even though none of us knew him well. As the years passed and the occasional rumor came down that Mark and the others had been killed or that a lead had opened up, I knew that at some point my kids might have to face the news that for all of our praying, Mark would never see his family again. And that is exactly what happened. It was particularly hard to hear conclusively in 2001 that they had already been dead five years.

Global engagement has to have a face. Or rather a multitude of faces. Our community of greater Milwaukee is not, culturally speaking, a cosmopolitan area. There is cultural and ethnic diversity, but with a lot of segregation. You could grow up here with your entire world being an area within a ten-mile radius of your home. But it doesn't have to be that way for us, or for any church anywhere.

Fostering a global perspective in a church and leading people into real engagement with the world are what saves us from a stunted, constricted understanding of the gospel. Engaging the world is not a matter of writing a check in an impersonal and condescending way to some needy area about which, truth be told, we'd really rather not know the details.

Later in the book when we look at global engagement, I will describe how the members of our churches can become personally invested in the lives of other believers and churches in faraway places, and with specific groupings of nonbelievers. Those personal connections develop through effective storytelling, mutual ministry, short-term overseas ministry, and other means. Most important, the kind of global perspective that will both burden and liberate us will come through an understanding and experience of the greater work of God, through a real conviction that in the body of Christ there is no one greater than another, no one who can say he or she doesn't belong, and no one who excludes someone whom God includes.

Every church can be a Whole Church. And every Whole Church will be a global church.

IN PRACTICE—COHESIVE IDEAS
FOR A WHOLE CHURCH
----

1. Plan now how you might pass along the idea of engagement to other leaders in your church.[1]
2. Begin to think now about how to introduce the idea of engagement to everyone in your church.[2]
3. Communicate with passion what a Whole Church can be. Don't just teach about unity in the church. Demonstrate a longing for and enthusiasm about unity wherever it can be found.
4. Frequently celebrate stories of engagement. Tell the stories of people who were transformed by a mission trip they went on, who were supported in a time of crisis by people in the church, who discovered the power of the Word of God for the first time.
5. Begin two lists right now—one of examples of engagement in your church, another of possible ideas for future engagement for your church—and develop them as you read this book. Expand those lists as you work through this book.
6. Read Ephesians and 1 Corinthians sometime in the next couple of weeks. Note ideas of engagement (especially in the idealism of Ephesians) and examples of fragmentation (especially in 1 Corinthians).
7. List twenty examples in your church of where you have seen God's supply brought together with human need in the last year or two.
8. Reflect on funerals you have been part of where God's supply met human need.
9. Make note of every time someone expresses gratitude for grace and truth they found in the church. Let those moments be markers.
10. Honestly assess where your own attitude is toward your church today: grateful? committed? worried? hurt? bitter? afraid? enthusiastic? confused?
11. Avoid generalizing about your church. Every church has mature and immature people, moments of the Whole Church and episodes of fragmentation, leaders who are divisive and leaders who instinctually bring people together.
12. Release to God any anger or resentment you have toward your church. Ask God to give you a picture of the church as a bride.

13. Make a mental note before going further in this book: Which of the four kinds of engagement come most easily for your church? Which with the most difficulty? Which are central to your church's life, and which are undiscovered?
14. Make a decision to personally commit to engagement on all four levels.
15. Ask yourself how many time-consuming activities in the church contribute absolutely nothing to engagement. They have nothing to do with bringing divine supply together with human need.
16. Talk to two or three other leaders in your church about what sense of calling they have about your church. Are they open to the idea of engagement?
17. In the worship time of your church, make some notes over the next four weeks of the moments when there seems to be a true engagement with God.
18. You are probably talking in your church about these four kinds of engagement, but in your own language. Write down the language your church culture uses for each of the four.
19. If your church is not promoting engagement in one or more of these ways, take some time and prayer to figure out why that may be.
20. Make a note now of which leaders in your church you will want to talk with in the weeks to come, and in what context you will talk, about the ideal of Whole Church.
21. Ask God to open your eyes to examples of your church's engaging at one of these four levels. Don't be discouraged; discover what already is happening and how that can lead to next steps.
22. Subscribe to a church leaders' e-mail list of your choice in order to get a continual flow of encouraging ideas.
23. Foster a friendship with someone who is a church leader like yourself from a different church in town. Support each other in your work.
24. When you get to be around other church leaders outside your own, ask questions relentlessly. Don't wait to find the perfect church paradigm to import. Infuse your church with specific concrete ideas that will develop your church's culture.
25. Talk to a friend or family member who is not a church leader about what your hopes and frustrations in ministry are right now.

PART TWO

FOUR KINDS
OF ENGAGEMENT
FOR THE
TWENTY-FIRST-CENTURY
CHURCH

4

ENGAGE WITH GOD

CLOSING THE GOD GAP THROUGH WORSHIP AND TEACHING

THE BIG IDEA

If a church does not come together when it gathers together, that is a sign of fragmentation. The practice of corporate worship is typically a church's best chance to bring people together, developing values and experiences that hold a church together. That is most likely to happen when the focus of worship and preaching is an authentic engagement with God.

ONE GOOD FRIDAY

In our part of the world, the Good Friday worship gathering is always one of the most moving experiences of the year. Of course, that is not because of what we do, but because it is an authentic engagement with God. The people come with this mind-set: *bring us together with the crucified Jesus. We know it is hard; we know that if we let the reality of this sink in, our hearts will be broken. But let them break. We know this is right. That's why we've come.*

I don't think I'm reading that into people's minds. I've watched it happen for almost thirty years.

People come to the 1 PM service or 7 PM service with an appropriate soberness. The lights are dimmed; twenty yards of black cloth are draped on the cross on the back wall of the sanctuary and spread out from there across the platform. A crown of thorns might be sitting on a pedestal. Stringed instruments play as people gather, their voices sending a solemn message.

We sing songs about and to the crucified Lord. There is no rush. The service is simple and respectful. There may be slides projected at different points with verses of Scripture or images of the Passion. The sound of a hammer hitting a spike comes from some hidden place. At some point, a part of the Passion story is read from the Gospel of Luke. The sound of that hammer and spike seems to have more of an impact than anything visual in the whole service.

The message is succinct. And there is usually an invitation to participate in some way. A couple of years ago, we handed, with no explanation, a large nail to everyone as he or she entered the service. People held that uncomfortable bit of hardware through the whole service. Their hands gradually began to smell metallic. Occasionally a person accidentally dropped his or her nail on the concrete floor, making a conspicuous "ch-ching." That was unanticipated, but not a problem. Worship should not be entirely predictable. I remember thinking that the crucifixion was not orderly, so our Good Friday worship should not be meticulous either.

But the thing I will never forget is the end of that service. After teaching about the effects of the sacrifice of Jesus and the promise of forgiveness, I told the congregation that I didn't want them to have to go home with the cruel nail they were holding. So they should leave it. Better yet, if they didn't need to rush off, I invited them to come forward to the front and pitch their nail at the base of the specially erected cross on the platform beneath which the black cloth flowed. I thought that maybe half of the people would step forward and that the others would just leave their nails in their seats, go to their cars, and drive back to work or home.

But quietly, slowly, and intentionally, every person came forward. It took more than twenty minutes for all twenty-five hundred people there to step forward. Some tossed their nail, a look of confession on their faces. Others threw the nail with force, as though they were casting guilt straight out of their minds. Some stopped and prayed before tossing their nail. Parents brought their children with their own nails. Someone helped a man in a wheelchair get up on the platform itself so that he could get close to the cross and rid himself of the nail.

It wasn't long before the cloth was covered with nails, so each successive nail made a loud "ting-ching" as it fell against others. Dozens of nails were being tossed almost simultaneously, so for most of that twenty minutes the sound was continual—no more individual sounds, but a river of sound that filled the whole room. It was overwhelming. It produced in me a conflicted sensation of pain and relief. And when the last nails were thrown and most of the people had left in silence, many others went back to their seats and stayed another half hour in silent prayer or tears.

I use this example not in order to make the point that we can help people through creative worship planning (which is true). I use it because it is a pure example, I think, of worship as engagement with God. This was not about me the preacher; or our worship pastor, who had planned a beautiful and haunting music set; or our worship assistant, who set the whole platform in a memorable way. This was about the people and their Lord. We just set the table; he provided the meal.

And I remember thinking that day, and then that Easter, *Wouldn't it be great if we could take moments of connection with God and just lock ourselves in? Here is the church being what the church is supposed to be—like the picture of the worshipping church in Revelation. Let's just stay right here, because on this day we got it right.*

But, of course, you can't stay there, any more than a marriage is defined by the day of the wedding. Engagement with God is a movement. Each week holds new possibilities, but also new potential for fragmentation.

ENGAGING WITH GOD THROUGH TRANSFORMATIONAL WORSHIP

Worship is intended to be a rhythm or pattern of life with an ever-compounding effect in a believer's life. Many have written in recent years about transformational worship. The proposition offered here is this: the pattern of public worship is transformational insofar as it is an authentic engagement with God. That may sound obvious, but because we are entirely capable of "doing worship" in ways that come nowhere close to God, or that come close but are hesitant to engage, we have to commit to the work of creative and deep thinking in our planning for worship.

But let's get concrete so that we don't just linger in the theory. We know that worship in the local church, at its worst, can be lifeless, rote, vacuous, cliché (an insult to both divine and human nature), selfish, prejudicial, exploitative, manipulative, dehumanizing, or idolatrous—in other words, "false worship," an expression that should strike fear into us. No wonder churches are capable of displaying as much fragmentation as any other human association. We are capable of taking our highest moment—the worship encounter—and turn it into an isolating experience.

Worship is dangerous. Just think of the apostle Paul telling the church in Corinth that their gatherings were so destructive that it would probably be better if they didn't meet (1 Cor. 11:17). Imagine putting an announcement in a church bulletin that said, "Due to the fact that we are doing more harm than good, we will no longer be gathering for worship, effective immediately." Of course, churches don't need to close themselves down—people take care of that on their own. They walk away, leaving a core group that is very happy living as one extended dysfunctional family.

We can do better. And we won't do better necessarily by working harder or acquiring a new model of worship. What needs to happen is for us as church leaders to have a vision for engagement with God in worship and to be committed to that absolutely. Again, let's get concrete. Engagement with God in worship looks like . . .

A song, "In Christ Alone," that marches people through a progression of spiritual truth, carried on a tune that is singable and consistent with the tone and the meaning of the words

A prayer offered by a young woman who has a gift of faith and who flourishes in prayer, who is aware of leading the congregation, but far more aware of the presence of God

A pastor explaining the offering as an act of worship because it is an act of honoring God, with an ancient biblical history

A sermon that engages because it brings God's supply (the word of truth) into contact with real human need (including practical application), leaving people with a sense that they heard from God, not just from a speaker

A personal word from a former police officer who at one time despaired of his life, but who found Christ at the low point of his depression

A "gathering time" before the worship service that is ten minutes of singing, helping people shift from their normal lives to a true engagement with God

A led prayer at the end of a worship service with quiet moments that allow people to open themselves to God before leaving and reentering the rush of normal life

A time of communion where extra time is allotted to allow for more meditation

A sense of anticipation because there is usually one creative element in the worship time that could be almost anything (a personal story, a video message or illustration, an interview with a missionary, a dramatic sketch)

Creativity in worship is important, although "being creative" does not mean that worship has to be a major production. Some of the most creative elements are very simple. More important is engagement. Does every element of worship seek to connect divine supply and human need? And is that the motive of the people who are leading the time of worship?

WORSHIP AS A WHOLE-CHURCH PATTERN

Worship has always been and will always be one of the most significant points of engagement between God and his people. Today's ongoing experimentations with worship are a sign that we know we still have to find a communal way to engage with God that is true and faithful. Our drive to worship is clear: from the beginning of history to the end, from walking with God in Eden to the vision of all creation worshiping Christ in John's Apocalypse. There is such a drive to adore, to glorify, to exalt, to venerate, to revere—we die if we don't.

As a practical matter and as a principle, church leaders need to be on the same page about why they worship, how they worship, and what their expectations of worship are. We need to develop a common worship mind-set and keep reinforcing it. To be a Whole Church, we have to see the act of worship as a prime time when the people of the church are pulled together—although we have to be honest and acknowledge that worship is so personal, so powerful, and so important that individuals will always have mixed opinions about what their leaders in worship are doing for them or to them.

Here are three of the dynamics of worship: *purposes, practices,* and *effects.* We may be most aware of the effects (or noneffects), as we are very human, and tend to think nothing matters more than our experience. But the best way to promote authentic worship is to begin at a higher level. The diagram illustrates that at the top of a pyramid of priorities, most important, are the purposes of worship. Then we get to the practices of worship—which must be

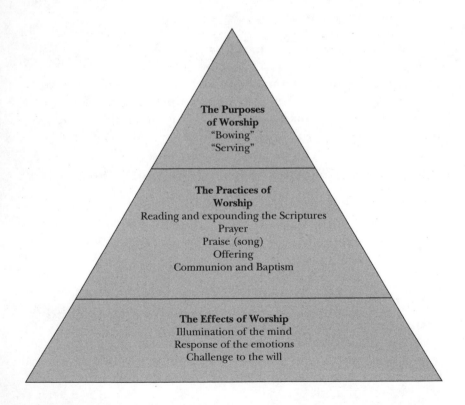

**The Purposes
of Worship**
"Bowing"
"Serving"

**The Practices of
Worship**
Reading and expounding the Scriptures
Prayer
Praise (song)
Offering
Communion and Baptism

The Effects of Worship
Illumination of the mind
Response of the emotions
Challenge to the will

carried out with integrity. And finally come the effects of worship. People will talk most about the effects, but church leaders need to start with biblical purposes so that the eventual effects of worship are what God intends.

THE PURPOSES OF WORSHIP

Worship can be a powerfully cohesive force in a church and between churches if we understand and commit to the nonnegotiable biblical principles of worship. Two ideas emerge: worship as "bowing" and worship as "serving." Rooted as they are in biblical theology, these two principles can be conceived as God's invitation to engage.

Bowing or bending the knee (*gonupeteo,* from *gonu,* "knee") refers to the characteristic posture of a servant before a master. Solomon at the temple, Daniel in prayer, the whole assembly in the days of Hezekiah's revival—they all bent the knee, or bowed, before God in worship. One of the best things a worship leader or pastor can do for a church is to continually characterize all the practices of worship as acts of submission. Worship promotes the Whole Church because all worshipers are rehearsing the truth that we are less than the God we bow before, and more than the animals who don't know how to bow.

Archbishop William Temple defined worship in this way:

> Worship is the submission of all our nature to God. It is the quickening of conscience by his holiness; the nourishment of mind with his truth; the purifying of imagination by his beauty; the opening of the heart to his love; the surrender of will to his purpose—and all this gathered up in adoration, the most selfless emotion of which our nature is capable and therefore the chief remedy for that self-centeredness which is our original sin and the source of all original sin.

That's worth writing down and reading frequently, and the operative term is *submission,* which is the meaning of bowing or bending the knee.

Singing is submission (praise that looks up); prayer is submission (bringing cares and confession to God on high); listening to a sermon is submission (putting the structures of our lives under the authority of Scripture); the public reading of Scripture is submission (receiving the counsels of God); offering is submission (bringing gifts to the gift-giving God). There are hundreds of ways a leader can signal to a congregation that they are submitting to God in everything that is done in worship. And if that lifetime pattern is set and the mind-set developed, then worship will transform.

The other main biblical word for worship is "service" (*latreuo* and *leitourgos* in the New Testament). In the Old Testament, the priestly pattern of worship was the service of the altar. The New Testament acknowledges that (Heb. 8:5; 9:1, 6, 9, 14; 10:2; 12:28; 13:10), but then goes beyond to show that the service of God is a seven-day-a-week opportunity (as in Rom. 12:1: "to offer your bodies as living sacrifices . . . your spiritual act of worship").

How many of our problems with worship would be mitigated if we remembered that we don't worship for our sakes, but as a pattern of honor to God? Don't slide over this point. Given human nature, we know that church congregations will always tend to measure the validity of worship by its effect on them. Cultures based on commercialism will even (unconsciously) view worship as a product. But the core of mature believers in a church really can be called to a higher standard. We can challenge people on this point: Don't we believe that rehearsing submission to God with all of our being is the life-transforming pattern we need? Let joy and enthusiasm happen when they will. The "aha moments" of learning from God may happen days or weeks or even longer after a given worship experience.

So instead of asking, "Are we worshiping yet?" (and then proceeding to have an argument about what kind of music is true worship, and what the content of the message should be), the better question is, "Would God say that he was worshiped in this place today?"

Does it matter to God if the song we sing is two hundred years or two years or two days old? Would God call a gathering "true worship" if the clothing of the worshipers were more formal or more comfortable? And what about our state of mind? Is God worshiped only when we have a certain mental or emotional state during the act of worship? What does that have to do with the service of God and submission to God? If our subjective experience were the true measure of worship, then the grieving man whose father just died on Tuesday could not worship, nor could the teenage girl who is coming down with the flu, the music instructor who is distracted by the fact that the worship guitarist doesn't have his guitar tuned perfectly, the believers who gather in secret places because of persecution and who dare not sing above a hush, or the believers who dare not gather with more than two or three people at a time.

Dare we say that people only "truly" worship when certain criteria are met? Isn't it God who should say, "I was worshiped by that person in that place today"?

THE PRACTICES OF WORSHIP

Worship must be rooted in principle, but it is a real act, a real engagement with God in every worship "practice." Despite the conspicuous differences in the way different churches worship, a core body of practices express the worship instincts of the Whole Church. They typically include reading and explaining the Scriptures, prayer, praise, communion, baptism, offering. You can be sitting in a five-hundred-year-old Anglican chapel with a small organ, old hymnals, and a stone baptistery, or under the spreading bows of an acacia tree in the hundred-degree weather of Southern Sudan, where young men with guitars that don't have all their strings are leading worship. You can go back in time to the early church meetings in homes, to the Wesleyan class meetings, to a "home church" meeting in a barn in the heart of China. We do what comes by instinct when we gather: read the Word, talk about it, pray, praise, and a few other things.

I am astonished and moved whenever I go to some Christian gathering very different from my own, and watch the mystery of corporate worship unfold—the praise, the word, the sacrament, the testimony—and I think, *I am part of this. I get to be part of this thing that connects believers all over the world.* The prayer of the Koreans overwhelms me. The exposition of the Scottish preacher challenges me. The celebration of the African American congregation loosens my spirit.

Now of course some churches add other creative elements, and some never physically take an offering in the gathering or do baptism in a nearby lake rather than in the worship auditorium. But the core practices are stable enough that we know that worship is one of the key dynamics of the Whole Church, and we must not let that be taken away by our own mistakes in the past.

Why does it matter that there are these core practices?

1.   *We are encouraged and emboldened* to be committed to worship when we see this incredible movement of God around the world and over the centuries. Only God could cause hundreds of millions of people each week to gather to pray, read Scripture, submit to Word-based direction, and perform other core worship practices. We can be cynical or discouraged when we focus on the differences and the flaws, but the big story of the day is that God is being worshiped.

2.   Understanding core practices should make us commit to *quality, honesty, and authenticity* when we carry them out. A prayer in a worship gathering should be taken very seriously—prepared in mind and heart. Every sermon holds the potential of having a transforming effect in someone's life, and in most people's lives it is the long pattern of being taught that makes the difference.

3.   Core practices of worship combined with the intentional purposes of submission and service give worship an *objectivity*. We do worship when we serve God in this way, not just when a certain effect happens in us. Worship will change us, but only if we make it not about us but about God. This must be said again and again because it is just so difficult for us (leaders and nonleaders) to get it: worship is about God, not primarily about us. When we believe that, then there will be effects in our lives.

THE EFFECTS OF WORSHIP

If people have a mind-set of submission and service and faithfully and creatively carry out the practices of worship, there will be effects. This is the personal experience: the illumination of the mind, the response of the emotions, a challenge to the will.

We tend to think first about our experience, and we will even judge the validity of worship by discerning the effects, but that is to start at the end. Worship is not validated by our experience. Our best chance at experiencing transformative worship is when our worship is rooted in an engagement with God (submitting and serving) and practiced as a regular pattern of life.

PREACHING AND THE WHOLE CHURCH

The time has come. The last person speaking or the last song sung has finished, and you step up in front of the crowd of people and begin speaking. It is a unique transitional moment in ministry. For as many times as I have done this—standing up to speak to a gathered group or crowd to teach—it still strikes me each time as mysterious, invigorating, and ominous all at the same time.

The speaker, teacher, or preacher[1] is helping people engage with God. What could be better than that? It cannot be said enough. The teaching-preaching ministry of a church holds the prospect of being one of the most significant powers in getting people to engage at every level—with God, with God's people, with the community, and with the world—as the teacher uses persuasive and enlightening words to move people out of their complacency toward the wider world outside.

If the purpose of preaching is to close the God gap, to be an instrument in bringing God's supply in contact with human need, then there are huge benefits . . .

We have clarity in what we are doing. We are released from the agony of measuring whether we are "successful" in the ministry of the Word, because the purpose of it all is to bring the Word to the people, and the people to the Word. Preaching is nothing if it is not a divine movement, a true engagement.

We don't measure short-term results. The faithfulness and effectiveness of any one message cannot be evaluated by the immediate response of the people through comments or CD sales. How many CDs would Jeremiah have sold of his oracles of woe? A sermon should call people to respond, but only God knows when and how that will happen. Do we or do we not believe Jesus' parable of the soils? The Word is planted, and with the passage of time, we find out whether any one person is good soil or thorny, shallow, or rocky. The teacher's job is to plant. Time will tell what happens as a result.

We avoid diversions that are a waste of energy and time. People may respond to preaching that is simple advice giving, but they can get that in a magazine in the grocery store line or the self-help section of the bookstore. They come to church to meet God. We get to help them do that. So why would we want to do anything else? Faithful preaching will address real-life issues, but we don't always decide what those issues are. The "hermeneutical circle" means that we can bring our questions to the text, but we at least as often begin with the text and let it pose the questions.[2]

AIMING AT THE CENTER IN PREACHING

If we are committed to engagement with God as the purpose of preaching, then what we must do is *aim at the center.* Whether the speaker is standing in front of a high school group, a men's breakfast, or a mixed group on Sunday morning, every person sitting there has layers to his or her life, but beneath all the layers is the core person—the center. The layers include social position, financial condition, education, relationships, age, family background, mental and emotional health or illness, generational culture, ethnic culture, prior spiritual experience. Given all the variables, every person is unique. How could we think otherwise? So why is it that so many "church experts" tell church leaders that they need to put people into categories and then minister to them in those boxes? Why would we think that the core issues of life—the real core, the true center—are any different for a young adult and a senior citizen? Yes, it surely is true that young adults today look for belonging and relationships, but do we believe that middle-aged people and children and senior citizens are not interested in belonging and relationships? Is it not likely that generational and cultural differences are matters of degree, not of kind?

If we want to help people engage with God when we teach them, we will aim at the center. This is what the Scriptures mean by the "heart." The core of a human being, the heart, is where opinions form, biases develop, bitterness festers. At the heart is the idealistic created soul that longs to find and follow God, and where temptation begins its work. The heart is the inner sanctum. It is the Holy of Holies. It is where people engage with God.

We will not have to worry about "relevance" if we aim at the center, because there is nothing more important to a person than the core issues of life. Here are some of the questions almost everybody wants to find an answer for:

Is there any purpose to my life?

How can I know I am forgiven?

How can I forgive the people in my life?

Will God ever give up on me?

Why are my bad habits so hard to break?

What can I do with my fears?

Whom can I count on?

What is God really like?

How do I know when God is speaking to me?

What should I do with my guilt?

Where do I belong?

How should I spend my time, energy, and resources in my life?

Why is there suffering in the world?

What should I believe? (the question of faith)

What is going to happen to me in the future? (the question of hope)

Does anyone care about me? (the question of love)

How can we better raise our kids?

Will I be financially secure in the future?

How can I lead a healthier life?

How can I know what to believe?

You could sit down right now and come up with twenty more. All you have to do is look into your own heart or read the Scriptures for an hour or two and jot down the core human issues that are brought front and center.

When I stand up in front of the crowd that is the worship service of our church, I feel invigorated and sometimes a bit anxious because I look out and see children and teens and young adults and middle-aged adults and older adults. I see some ethnic diversity (roughly the same diversity as found in the community in which we are located). I know there are some who are wounded and others who are hard-hearted. I am astonished that all these people have gathered in this place. And for a bit more than a half hour, I get to read and explain the Word to the Whole Church. That is when I want to be aware of who these people are—at the center.

What do you think? Is common human nature a small target or a substantial field of transformative ministry? Do we aim at the characteristics that distinguish people from each other, or do we aim at the essential core of the human soul?

The first of the two figures that follow (on p. 55) shows three diverse people; the field that they hold in common, essential human nature, is depicted as a very small target. This figure would suggest that we have to aim at what makes people different in order to connect with their humanity. The second figure (on p. 56) reflects the realm of the soul, essential human nature, as a substantial field of ministry. It emphasizes that most people living in most places at most times have the same core questions and concerns in life.

Taking the second view matters in two ways. First, you will "aim at the center" in the ministry, knowing that you can go for years working on essential questions people have (see the earlier list). Second, if you believe that the core of human nature is a substantial field, then you will have an easier time believing in the Whole Church. You will view "the body of Christ" as our reality, not just theory. You will believe that you can speak to a crowd of people different in age, gender, race, and temperament and be able to get them engaged with God and with each other.

When we aim at the center, these important things happen:

We speak to the human place where transformation happens (and where deformation began).

We bring God's supply to the center of need; we help people engage with God.

We bring the Whole Church together because diverse people can
see their common humanity.

We go deep (down to the level where real human problems lie),
and we go high (to the place where there are still vestiges of
the image of God).

I remember our high school football coach telling the quar-
terbacks, "Just aim at the numbers; aim at the numbers." What
he meant was, throw the football at the center of the torso of the

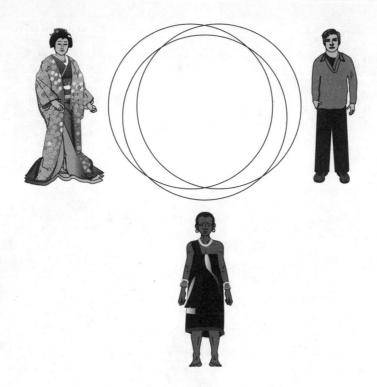

receiver, at the big numbers on the front of his jersey. I think of that frequently in ministry. Don't aim at where you think people should catch the ball—aim at the center of the person. That's the best way we have to connect.

- -

IN PRACTICE—COHESIVE IDEAS
FOR A WHOLE CHURCH

- -

1. Plan a time to teach your whole church about the purposes of worship (bowing and serving), but do so only after you have delved into and been inspired by the scriptural texts that form the background.
2. Make worship planning a group process; bring truly creative thought into the process.

3. Make sure that the person delivering the sermon or message is integral to the worship planning process.

4. Review the responses and comments from people in the church with the worship planning team. Don't take flattery too seriously, and don't get blown out of the water by scathing criticism. But look for the kernel of truth in every critique.

5. Ask all worship participants to prepare carefully, because they are stepping into a divine action.

6. Listen to the questions and responses of different kinds of people (those of different ages, genders, races and ethnic backgrounds, degrees of spiritual maturity). Ask people for specifics. Watch for those subjects that cut across the lines of the Whole Church.

7. Expect worship leaders to serve God to the best of their ability, while not being limited by an exaggerated idea of excellence imposed on them.

8. Make the effort to find worship songs that (a) are singable and (b) have real content.

9. If there is special lighting in the worship space, use it to bring all worshipers together. Don't be enslaved by stage lighting standards that intentionally isolate performers from audience.

10. Break down barriers between worship leaders and the congregation. Teach that God is the audience and that all worshipers (leaders and congregation) are before God in the act of worship.

11. Try alternating between topical series and sermon series that progressively work through books of the Bible.

12. For a change of pace, try doing a sermon series that takes a year to complete. Do not be limited to the common pattern of sermon series that are two to six weeks long. Most people come to church and are primarily concerned about what help is offered them through God's Word on that particular day.

13. Share a teaching series. It is not necessary for one person to deliver all the messages in a particular series. In fact, sharing a book study, for instance, is a way of reinforcing the unitive power of the Word for the Whole Church.

14. Each January, print a Scripture reading schedule that people can use to read through the Bible in a year.

15. Teach ministry leaders how to engage in meaningful prayer in all their meetings.
16. Introduce extemporaneous prayer into worship if your church is liturgical; introduce set prayers into worship if your church is informal.
17. Hand out a printed description of different Bible translations.
18. Insist that people who offer prayers in worship services avoid tired old clichés and jargon (this can be hard!). Make a list of code lingo that a newcomer would not understand, and talk about natural language substitutes.
19. Offer retreats for spiritual enrichment.
20. Have someone who is gifted in prayer give a personal testimony about how prayer has changed his or her life.
21. Recommend books on prayer.[4]
22. Take time in worship for the careful reading of Scripture. Make such readings deliberate, carefully paced, and dramatic.
23. Teach about the biblical idea of meditation; explain the ineffectiveness and superficiality of always running to the next thing.
24. Make spiritual disciplines integral to whatever premembership instruction is used, and at every age level of Christian education.
25. In preaching, let the enthusiasm of personal discovery come through strongly, modeling personal Scripture reading as a core pattern.

5

ENGAGE WITH GOD'S PEOPLE

CLOSING THE PEOPLE GAP THROUGH REAL *KOINONIA*

THE BIG IDEA
Engagement is a progressive divine act through which the closing of the God gap leads naturally to closing the people gap. Engagement between God's people is the essential dynamic whereby a church community is formed and individuals find their own authentic connections.

EXPERIMENTS IN COMMUNITY

Matthew is in his midtwenties. As he returns home from his job in the city, supper is on the stove, a large pot of spaghetti that will serve the six adults living in this classic old two-story home on the near north side of downtown. Matthew, one other single man, and two couples have been living in this house for the past two years as an intentional act of community and mission. They were in a Bible study together and came to a conviction that they wanted to learn what it means to live in community as Christ followers, and to live in a troubled part of the city as an act of Christian witness. They didn't have any particular plan; they just believed that being part of a neighborhood would lead to relationships out of which they could show the love of Christ. Two years into it, they still feel that they are finding their way. They have a steady stream of visitors who come by for prayer and discussion, but they are frustrated that most of their personal connections are still with people outside the neighborhood they are living in.

Janet and Jeff belong to and host a small group sponsored by their church. The couple follows a typical pattern: a weeknight meeting in their home where the agenda is Bible study or study of some other kind of reading, prayer, and general visiting with each other and catching up on their lives. It has been five years now that they have been meeting with about a dozen people. One year into it, they realized that they really were becoming a spiritual family. They leaned on each other when someone was sick or when one of their children was in trouble. When Janet had back surgery, the group was there to organize meals and cleaning for the family in her absence. At the start of the group, they had intended to serve in some way together as a group, but they have found that challenging. Bible study is easy, prayer comes naturally, and everybody loves the friendship of fellowship, but they just haven't gotten around to serving together in any regular way. Although part of the difficulty is the effort required, a big factor is that they are low on imagination and ideas of where they can go and whom they can serve. But they have recently found a connection with a local resale shop that supports the work of a crisis pregnancy center, and have committed to helping out at the center one Saturday a month. Serving together is now bringing them a freshness and energy they didn't have before.

Michael never thought he would be part of a small group with four other men. His career and his personal interests filled his life, and he always found relationships difficult. But at a Saturday morning prayer breakfast for men, he was challenged by the speaker, who asked how many men had a commitment to Christ but had no answer for what kind of a difference it was making in their lives. The follow-up was an invitation to do a four-week study with a small group of men on the topic of "making a difference." Michael didn't know on week one when he met with the four other guys at 6 AM for breakfast that at the end of the four-week run he would enthusiastically agree to continue meeting with the group for the next six months. The men in the group are following a discipleship curriculum that emphasizes spiritual disciplines and life in the marketplace. It also leads them into accountability to each other—something that they would not have agreed to at the start. For each of them, it was the first time they had talked about temptation and failure with anybody. They became aware that their safety net was not foolproof, however, when the group learned that one of them was having extreme difficulty in his marriage and no one else knew it.

IN SEARCH OF *KOINONIA*

In the last thirty years there has been a vigorous discussion among church leaders about building community in local churches, and many experiments along the way: small groups, house churches, missional communities. This revolution in ministry is a rediscovery of the dynamics enjoyed in earlier eras, including the house churches of the New Testament, the house churches of the Pietist movement in seventeenth-century Europe, the mission-minded small groups of the eighteenth-century Moravians, the class meetings of John Wesley, and so on. This should validate our commitment, as the very best dynamics of church ministry can't possibly be entirely new. "Innovation" means change in or renewal of something established. Precedence authenticates innovation.

In this chapter we will look at *engagement with God's people,* which is the natural consequence of engagement with God. Spiritual life and growth begin with closing the God gap by leading people into a life of engagement with God, and the next logical step is engagement with God's people. Becoming a body. Discovering community. Joining with brothers and sisters in Christ. Vertical engagement leading to horizontal engagement. Reconciliation with God leading to reconciliation with others. We start to live life in a Whole Church.

Engagement with God's people is the prodigal son realizing he has to figure out how to live with his brother. Coming home means you get your father back, and you get your brother back— whether you want him or not. Therein lies the opportunity and the difficulty of community. It is easy for church theorists to talk idealistically about the virtues of community, but the challenging reality is that although on our better days we get along with our brothers and sisters, on our worst days we fight with each other like children scrapping for toys or shoving their way to the front of the line. We want to humbly approach the throne of Jesus, but then we want to know who will sit at Jesus' right hand. We are never far away from the James and John syndrome.

Fragmentation happens easily because the cracks start in the depths of human nature. Sometimes we fragment like bitter family members who break off and flee, but sometimes we slowly and imperceptibly drift apart. We don't know we're fragmented until we notice that we're enveloped in silence; we look around and can't see anybody else. Church leaders have a special vulnerability here. We are supposed to be leading people into community, but leadership is frequently a lonely experience. Lonelier still if we, for whatever reason, separate ourselves from each other. Sometimes church leaders are more isolated from each other than are people in the congregation.

Scientific studies in the last ten to twenty years have established these two dynamics: society is becoming increasingly fragmented, and people are longing for real community. More than ten years ago, a Gallup Institute survey carried out under the direction of Dr. Robert Wuthnow of Princeton University revealed that 40 percent of Americans were involved in some kind of small group regularly (anything from a church group to a hobby group to a twelve-step program). Most of the people who said they were in a group (60 percent) were in some kind of faith-based group. Wuthnow called the small group movement "a quiet revolution" in American society. He also found that 71 percent of people in spiritually based groups said their experience helped them in the healing of relationships.[1]

Before we extol the virtues of community, we need to understand the fundamental dynamics of human disintegration. Organizational fragmentation is most of the time rooted in human fragmentation. Building community is not just a matter of herding people into a room and calling it community—it is to initiate a movement of relationships that access the power of God to reconcile. But what are we up against?

We're up against *partiality*. As human beings we control life by limiting ourselves to the fragments of life we prefer. We stick to our own group, become entrenched in our own limited opinions, build walls, define ourselves by what and whom we are against. There is a Catch-22 here for the church. We may find it easy to get people to join small subgroupings in the church (a good thing), but if ministries become silos, and believers only associate with people just like themselves, they miss the influence of the diversity of the body.

We're up against the aftereffects of *injury*. An injured animal will withdraw to a dark and isolated place and snap at anyone who approaches. People may seek each other out when injured, but may just as likely withdraw out of a primitive instinct to survive. Many wounded people show up at church, but cower in the corner as an act of self-preservation. We may need to let them do that for a while, but eventually they need their brothers and sisters.

We're up against *resentment*. It is no wonder people perk up when you talk about forgiveness. Everyone carries at least a little resentment, if not bitterness or even hatred. Grace and forgiveness are the hallmarks of the faith, but our instincts for fighting and resentment are never far away.

We're up against *ego*. "I" comes before "we." Leaders may have a need to stand out. We may, to the detriment of all, have to trumpet, "I have an idea" or "I get the credit."

We up against the dynamics of *control*. In Christ we find power and authority—both of which rescue and protect the wayward life. Historically, however, Christ-followers have too often institutionalized power and authority, and churches become control-based collectives. Heavy-handed engagement within a group without the liberating engagement with God leads to the development of a sect or faction or cult. Control is not the defining characteristic of community. Neither is control the hallmark of effective leadership.

We're up against *busyness*. Community? Sounds nice, but who has time for it?

It really is no wonder that we privatize faith. "Just you and me, God," is a whole lot easier than looking around and realizing that you've been adopted into a family whose members you did not choose. We want God's grace for ourselves, but we have questions about how generous God is with others (recall the parable of the same wage being paid to hired hands who worked different lengths of time, Matt. 20:1–16). It is too easy for us to forget that God's grace is our mission.

Any strategy that is effective in building community in a church must account for the dynamics of fragmentation. It would be nice if we didn't need to look at our embarrassing natures, but nobody benefits from naive or dishonest claims of community.

And consider this: we are living in an era when people are looking for connection and expecting authenticity at the same time, so gone are the days when a church can claim something that does not align with the way things really are. And that's a good thing. The only thing worse than no community is false community or empty rhetoric about community. Fellowship does not happen just by having a room in the church that is called Fellowship Hall. Worship does not automatically occur just by our calling an hour in the week a "worship service." We aren't experiencing brotherhood just by calling someone "brother."

THE SHARED LIFE: *KOINONIA* AS THE CONTROLLING PRINCIPLE

Community, simply put, is a matter of closing the people gap. If you ask the people in your church to make sure that they are engaging with each other, it is a true invitation to bring God's supply together with human need. "The eye cannot say to the hand, 'I don't need you!' And the head cannot say to the feet, 'I don't need you!' On the contrary, those parts of the body that seem to be weaker are indispensable, and the parts that we think are less honorable we treat with special honor" (1 Cor. 12:21–23). Engaging with God's people is another way of talking about the body of Christ acting like the body of Christ.

We need a controlling concept of community. We need a principle that transcends cultures and time and that will endure beyond the next decade. We will not find a better ideal than that of *koinonia*, the shared life. For most of us in most churches, we have only scratched the surface of what *koinonia* can mean.

Translated in various New Testament passages as "fellowship," "participation," "sharing," "partnership," and "communion," *koinonia* at its core means "the shared life" (the root *koin* means "common").

The first community after Pentecost dedicated themselves to their newly formed bond, "the fellowship," *koinonia* (Acts 2:42). *Koinonia* means the sharing of financial support ("the privilege of sharing in service"; "generosity in sharing," 2 Cor. 8:1–7). The church's proclamation is an offer of the shared life ("We proclaim to you what we have seen and heard, so that you also may have fellowship with us. And our fellowship is with the Father and with his Son, Jesus Christ." 1 John. 1:3).

The horizontal and vertical dynamics of "*koinonia* with us," and "*koinonia* with the Father and his Son" (note especially in 1 John) are prime examples of the exponential impact of different kinds of engagement. The shared life of believers rises directly out of shared life with God. There is in fact no real shared life of believers without the shared life of God. A church should not invite people into engagement with each other unless it is empowered and directed by engagement with God. *Koinonia* ministries succeed when the presence and power of God make them work.

THE COMPOUNDED POWER OF ENGAGEMENT

Remember that engagement is a movement, not a static state of being and not the categories of a program. Engagement with God and engagement with God's people both are continually unfolding divine acts through which divine supply is brought together with human need. And it is when we integrate both kinds of engagement that we see the power of God compounded in the church.

The following illustration shows, first of all, the undesirable situation of people relatively detached from God and from each other: *no engagement*. (The large circle represents God; the smaller circles, people.) A church may actually promote "no engagement" unintentionally if it offers no substantial way for people to connect with each other or if its approach to God is superficial, tentative, or agnostic. "No engagement" may also be the case if a church plays the church game—going through the motions, but not tying into the life of the Spirit. There is only one way to get out of the church game: an engagement with God that smashes the idols we build.

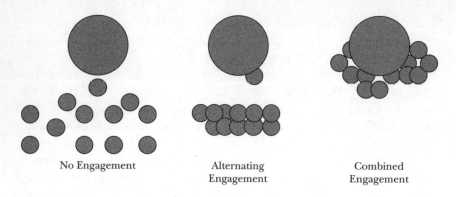

No Engagement   Alternating   Combined
                         Engagement   Engagement

The second possibility is what we could call *alternating engagement,* which occurs when a church encourages people to have a strong personal connection with God and promotes some kind of community connection, but keeps these elements of spiritual life separate. We meet with God, and we meet with others. We alternate between the vertical and the horizontal. People go to worship where there is little human connection, or they go to a group where there is little divine connection. We promote a deep personal connection with God, and we offer many opportunities for the body to gather. But we don't shape people engagement with divine engagement.

A theology of divine imminence (while taking nothing away from divine transcendence) leads to a different scenario for the full spiritual life.

We experience *combined engagement* when we see this all as one great divine movement. It is God bringing together what has become fragmented, and doing that work comprehensively— a human being connecting with God, then connecting with other human beings, the vertical combined with the horizontal not just in theory but in practice. This is that great work called *reconciliation.* As it says in Colossians 1:18–20, God "was pleased . . . to reconcile to himself all things, whether things on earth or things in heaven." Then the vertical switches to the horizontal: we have "the ministry of reconciliation" and "the message of reconciliation." We implore people to "be reconciled to God" and to be reconciled to each other. Even the simple little illustration here, which shows God in and with and among his people, is a way of describing that great movement begun in the incarnation.

"Combined engagement" means that we bring into our *koinonia* with each other the *koinonia* we have with God. We experience not just the shared life of humans, but the shared life of Christ.

SHORT-TERM TASK GROUPS AS ENGAGEMENT

Koinonia, the shared life, can happen in many different kinds of groups that have different purposes and different durations, and that are of different composition. The shared life is dynamic. It can happen in an instant, as when people are thrust together by a tragic event, or it can develop as a slowly emerging friendship. *Koinonia* can't be put in a box. It is what gets us out of the box of the stunted view of spiritual life.

One of the most formative kinds of group experiences is the twenty-four-hours-a-day immersion of a group in a significant mission. It may be a week or a month in duration. But if the task is well defined, the project carefully planned, and the team intentionally chosen, this *koinonia* moment can open people to a whole new life posture of engagement.

In the aftermath of Hurricane Katrina, which devastated New Orleans in 2005, one woman at Elmbrook Church decided she needed to do something. Watching the scenes of devastation on television was overwhelming, but also isolating. How could a person help when it seemed that the federal government couldn't even figure out how to intervene quickly in the situation? Within a few days after the hurricane, a team of fifteen people was heading to a small town in Mississippi with a semi-trailer truck of supplies that the church had gathered. As the group members drove deeper into the surreal landscape, they witnessed the indescribable: a land laid flat, bare foundations of homes with not a piece of lumber in place, trees flat on the ground like the corpses on a Civil War battlefield, cars crumpled and piled up against the walls of ditches.

The team was able to get in quickly because someone at Elmbrook knew one of the pastors of a small local Baptist church—a tenuous connection, but all that was needed to begin engagement. That is the difference between government assistance and the ministry of service-minded churches. Bureaucracy drops heavy tonnage of assistance by parachute. Churches can bring grace in hand door to door.

That is what happened during that week in Biloxi, Mississippi. Blankets, water, food, and clothing were dispensed on long tables outside the semi truck. But just as important, Wisconsin eyes met Mississippi eyes. Hands were shaken. The most frequent comment was, Why would a church in Wisconsin come way down here to Mississippi?

Almost more important than the distribution of goods was the opportunity the traumatized people of Biloxi had to tell their stories to members of the visiting team. "I was in my house when the water started rising . . ." "My dog is gone . . ." "My sister's boy is still missing . . ."

The members of the team had no feelings of heroism. Each one felt that he or she was doing so little, offering so little. And at the end of the week, each felt that he or she had received more than given.

The most important part of this story, however, is what happened in the three years following (and still to this day). Team 2 went a month after the first team. The situation was changing now, so there was more clean-up work. Eventually teams consisted of painters, drywallers, roofers, electricians, plumbers. People laid sod, repaired screens, installed floor tile, cleaned up debris, and cooked meals for workers. Team 3 went the month after that. Teams 4, 5, and 6 went in the following months. Team 17, arriving two years after Katrina, consisted of college students. Team 24 returned to Elmbrook three years after the hurricane.

This kind of long-term commitment develops with the compounding effect of engagement. The Katrina teams are not just one subprogram of a subprogram in the church. They constitute a true movement, engagement with the community (and, given the great distance, with the world, practically speaking) compounded with a powerful engagement of God's people with each other in eager service. And all this made worship on the ground in Biloxi of a depth and quality that is rare.

This is just one example of a short-term task group. There is an almost unlimited variety of short-term ministries groups can do. But they must be carefully conceived and responsibly prepared. There can be disappointing experiences with short-term groups, most often for two reasons: (1) the group goes to a location to perform a task, but the situation or task has not been adequately prepared (for example, a group went to a small town in Africa to erect a building, but the materials had not arrived); or (2) the group members are poorly chosen and their relationships poorly defined, so there is tension and conflict in the group.

Short-term task groups are a prime example of different kinds of engagement working together:

The Katrina group *engaged with God* by having frequent and urgent prayer before, during, and after the trip. As the team members sat in the small Baptist church in worship on their last night there, the sorrow of the tragedy and the joy of the human connection flowed out in worship. The project demonstrated engagement with God also in that it was a grassroots movement. No senior staff member thought it up. It began with one person watching a natural disaster on television and having a broken heart.

The group *engaged with God's people* by putting themselves in vans, sleeping in the pews of the church, hearing from each other about their families—and doing all the same things with their newfound friends in Biloxi. Church members who go on a mission together will often experience more *koinonia* in a week or two than they typically experience in a year or two.

The group *engaged with the community* (that is, our community at the home base in Wisconsin) by gathering supplies from local vendors and telling the story of Biloxi to other local groups. Upon their return, the local newspaper and a television station carried the story of the mission. A small group of people set out on a ministry of mercy, having no idea that their action would be broadcast in their hometown, a city of a million.

The whole project has also led to *engagement with the world.* Many members of the Katrina teams have sought other short-term ministry experiences, some of them who have never been out of the United States now getting a view of God's work in the world as they have joined other teams venturing out to foreign destinations. Once people get out of their bubble and into the wider world, the mission can be ten miles or a hundred miles or five thousand miles away.

The surest sign of real engagement is that it defies explanation. A divine movement is always beyond human words. The leaders of the Katrina teams say, There is no way of describing what we saw in Mississippi, and there is no way of describing the depth of love exchanged with our newfound friends there.

That is how you know that something has happened that is beyond our plans and programs. You hear the same thing from a group of students who travel to Mexico to work in an orphanage, a young adult group that volunteers one night a week at a residential home for the disabled, or a Bible study group that serves food twice a month at a local rehab center.

HOME FELLOWSHIP GROUPS AS ENGAGEMENT

The small group movement today has taken many forms, but one of the most portable, doable, high-impact forms is the home fellowship group. In the last thirty years, thousands of churches have begun these groups. Some pastors have been hesitant about initiating home fellowship groups, worrying that they can lead to fragmentation, when exactly the opposite is true. Lead people into a quality connection with brothers and sisters in a small group, and that engagement will only enhance engagement with the wider church.

The following are the typical contours of a home fellowship group:

A weekly meeting in someone's home

A pattern in which group members become more and more familiar with each other, growing in friendship

A ministry to each other during good times and bad—especially when crisis hits

An agenda that includes Bible study or some other discussion, sharing what is going on in each others' lives, and prayer

A fairly stable membership (some groups are fixed, others are open to newcomers, but home fellowship groups tend to coalesce around a central core of regular participants)

I have been part of a home fellowship group almost continu-ously since I was a teenager. The first one was the group that met at Dan and Bev's house on Friday nights. It is where I learned about group Bible discussion and heartfelt prayer. Twenty or so people sat around the perimeter of the longish living room with the memorable shag rug, the fireplace crackling to take the chill out of the air, the clink of coffee cups in their saucers. The discus-sion was pretty freewheeling, focusing on personal reaction and response to the biblical text. Week after week, month after month, I was being trained in Bible application. I was also being mentored by people twice and three times my age, though I didn't know the word "mentor" at the time.

In college, when our church announced that "neighborhood groups" were being formed, I assumed I should join in, though I was the youngest member of the group that met in the Erickson home, and one of the few unmarried. Our church was getting larger, and more people were falling through the cracks. The lead-ers of the groups were charged with providing learning, prayer, worship, and service. The first three came easy; service was always something that could slip. The neighborhood groups were the first line of spiritual and pastoral care—and that, I came to believe, was the real genius of the home fellowship group. No wonder peo-ple have described home fellowship groups as "churches within churches."

The group to which my wife and I have most recently belonged formed twenty years ago. In this case, my wife and I sought the fellowship of several other pastors and leaders (twelve in all) who could not easily share intimate personal details of their lives with just anybody in the church without making things very complicated. The group includes members from three different churches, meeting every other Sunday evening. We have watched our children grow up, praying for them across the years. We have prayed for each other when things are calm and stormy.

A lot of churches try small groups, and they just don't seem to work out. Like most ministry initiatives we try, we need to accept the reality that some things pan out and others don't. But if small groups did not work out in your church, it doesn't mean you can't give them another try, recognizing some of the reasons they didn't work out in the first place. Here are some essentials in properly preparing the ground:

1.   Have a clearly defined purpose for the groups. If "engaging with God's people" is the main thing your church needs to accomplish, then keep that focus. We as leaders must foster the shared life, *koinonia*. It is not just an option. We know that people will be better off when they can minister to each other, and not just depend on the pastor(s) of the church. Make *koinonia* a top priority, as the church did in Acts 2 ("they devoted themselves to 'the fellowship'"). Then build around that central purpose other things, such as Bible study, worship, and service.

2.   Recruit leaders who have the right gifts for leading a group. Here is where a lot of us get stuck. We look around and perceive that shortage of leaders that all churches do. We'll stay frozen there unless we take a calculated risk and designate people with real leadership potential, even though they themselves may not see it yet. A home fellowship group does not need a talented preacher, a seminary professor, or a professional musician to lead singing. The essential need is a person or a couple who are good hosts and facilitators. The leader or leaders need to have a genuine care for others and an instinct to draw out of others their strengths and weaknesses. Small group leaders need to be selfless in character. No one benefits from having his or her group leader be someone who wants to be the master of a small group of disciples. I once had to tell an overly ambitious group leader, "We already have a Master."

3.   Ease people into groups. Start groups by setting up a limited-term study of some pressing topic so that new people know they are committing to no more than a few meetings and for a very relevant purpose. For instance, offer a six-week small group experience in homes for people wanting to follow up a sermon series on discipleship. Or offer a four-week series on marriage and family issues, or on the matter of personal finance. There are more and more excellent curriculum packages available for small groups. Then groups can

offer a continuation of the group on another topic. If people had a good experience in the first sequence, they will consider extending their involvement in the group. They will have gotten over their fear and hesitation. After just a few meetings, they will feel that they have found new friends.

4. Give people a sense that they are "charter members." Some groups that are open will effectively accept newcomers, but churches often find that this produces just a trickle of people into groups. It is much easier to get disconnected people to consider joining a group if they feel as if it is a fresh start and that everybody in the group will be charter members with them. Everyone has natural hesitation about joining a group, and if they feel as if they have to break into a group that may not accept them, the barrier may be too high. Being on the same footing with everyone else, being part of a new thing, lowers at least one of the barriers.

I frequently ask myself, *Are the people in our church engaging with each other in true* koinonia? I know that it is one of the most essential things to aim at. My heart aches for people who are lonely and disconnected—we cannot look away. But *koinonia*, the shared life, is no less important for people who aren't convinced that they need it.

I could choose to answer the question by counting how many people are in small groups, but that is not the whole story, and there are many people who are in groupings that are not organized by the church. In the end, *koinonia* is a movement of God that is bigger than we are. It happens in small groups (although not automatically), but it also happens in friendships, work groups, interest groups, retirement homes, and happenstance connections. *Koinonia* even happens in large group settings when the Whole Church gathers, as when a thousand people experience something in a worship time that binds them together. *Koinonia* is God's work; we can set up the structures, but even more important is for us to set the values and the culture because the engagement of God's people is not our idea. It is God's mandate.

IN PRACTICE—COHESIVE IDEAS
FOR A WHOLE CHURCH

----

1. If your church has some kind of annual congregational meeting, transform it from a church business meeting into a time of celebration. If your tradition is to have a meeting that is full of deflating complaints, decide that things will be different the next time.

2. To transform an annual meeting into a congregational celebration, fill it with the stories of God's work in and through your church. Get the stories out by testimony or interviews.

3. Bring other leaders on board with a new kind of annual meeting by including them in the planning process.

4. If your church does not have an annual congregational meeting, start one, but give it a better name. Call it a vision night or celebration night.

5. At the annual meeting, leave the congregation with a clear picture of ministry focus for the year to come.

6. Make financial giving a cohesive dynamic in your church. Tell the stories of what happens when people give, and celebrate what happens when financial goals are achieved. A message of "look what God helped us accomplish together" has a mighty cohesive power.

7. Identify a few individuals who have a drive and gift to minister in practical ways. The next time there is a significant local tragedy (or a natural disaster in some other area), empower them to take a task group on a ministry of mercy.

8. Collect the stories of groups that do mercy ministry together. Give a spokesperson time in a worship service to tell the story of what God did through the group.

9. Tell those same stories in print, whether in the regular church newsletter or an occasional special mailing.

10. To begin new home fellowship groups, designate a time during the year to have an entry point for people not previously plugged in. This may, for example, be a four- to six-week group experience beginning in September tied into the sermons given during that time.

11. If you are just getting small groups going in your church, don't reinvent the wheel, but don't arbitrarily adopt a small group model of ministry either. There are many new books on developing small groups in churches.[2] Absorb what they are saying, and decide on a realistic path for your church.

12. When introducing or teaching about the Lord's Supper, expand on 1 Corinthians 10, which speaks of the "one loaf" and the "one body." Make a clear connection for people between reconciliation to God through Jesus, and reconciliation with each other.

13. Challenge small groups to engage in deep and substantive discussions (whether it is Bible study or topical discussions). Small groups are an opportunity for people to stretch their thinking, test ideas with each other, and apply principles to real life.

14. Train small group leaders (any kind of small group) in how to have a rich life of group prayer.

15. Arrange for some people to pray with those who have personal needs after a worship service.

16. Offer a group discussion guide pertaining to the topic of the sermon each week, enabling groups to apply what was gained in worship.

17. Seed a new church plant by having home groups meet for worship, teaching, fellowship, and service.

18. Occasionally or regularly have people greet others sitting around them at the start of a worship service.

19. Conclude a worship service with the words "Greet someone you don't know before you leave." (This seems like a small thing, but it creates an amazing connection between people and causes a buzz in the whole room.)

20. Have a small group give a "group testimony" in a worship service, speaking enthusiastically about how God works through community.

21. Use any auxiliary space around a worship center or sanctuary for interaction among people. Design points of contact or set up seating groups. Encourage lingering before and after worship.

22. Foster a *koinonia* culture early. Form a plan with children's ministry such that children learn about their connections with

each other, and even learn from each other by using small groups in classes, for instance.

23. Develop a strategy with the youth ministry on how best to foster a *koinonia* culture. Students have a desire for connection, but with every passing generation there are new challenges (for example, building trust in an age of broken families). Don't take a cookie-cutter approach.

24. Consider this possibility for youth, which has worked well at Elmbrook Church: a weeknight high school meeting at the church one time a month ("Insight") and a coming together in small groups in homes three times a month ("Outasight"). Students will feel a high degree of loyalty to the home groupings.[3]

25. If you are not in a *koinonia* context yourself, get into one. Find a situation that works for you, and model what you promote.

ENGAGE WITH YOUR COMMUNITY

MORE THAN A THOUSAND POINTS OF LIGHT

THE BIG IDEA

One of the most exciting developments in churches today is the renewed interest in engaging with the communities in which they are located, doing good deeds and forging relationships because these things are inherently valuable and give glory to God. When churches become missional in this local expression, they are taking on an essential part of the whole mission for the Whole Church, and they see their members engaging with each other, which is a powerful cohesive force.

John said that he didn't feel as though he had anything to offer the disadvantaged people who may wander into the storefront ministry sponsored by his church in his city. His skills didn't seem to fit; he didn't view himself as a counselor in any way. But volunteering at the front desk seemed safe. Two months later, he found himself one of the counselors pointing people to the parish nurse in the back room, to a financial counselor, to social services, or to a Bible study group. He did not realize that his perceived limitations in the "skills" of community engagement were based on a set of false assumptions—and fear. Now he cherishes every hour that he gets to be an advocate for disadvantaged people in his city.

When believers are truly engaged with God in a life of worship and devotion, and then engaged with each other in the shared life, the essentials are in place for the church's mission to be strong and vigorous. These believers are ready for engagement in their communities. But this engagement must be intentional, for it is all too easy for people who have been active participants in their neighborhoods, schools, businesses, and community organizations to withdraw from those connections when they become believers. They huddle in the church, treating it as an enclave rather than remaining in their communities as salt and light. What a shame. What an irony. People receive the gospel, their lives are transformed by its power, and then, when they have the opportunity to be transforming agents in the world, they withdraw. And we church leaders are often to blame—we tend to like the enclave, too.

Church leaders blow the trumpet, but are sometimes unaware that the signal is "Retreat!" rather than "Charge!" How does that happen? By building programs in the church that help believers engage with other believers (a good thing), but *without* setting down pathways of community engagement. We summon people to Fellowship Hall but not Fallen World. We bring them into Bible study groups but prompt them to withdraw from clubs and neighborhood associations. We even send signals that because they have new friends in the church, they can (or even should) discard old friends. We think of the "differentness" of holiness as disassociation from people and communities rather than disassociation from sin.

WHY DO WE WITHDRAW?

We need to understand the dynamics of community *dis*engagement so that we stop fragmenting our connections with our communities. Again, as is the case with other examples of fragmentation, the essential reason we disengage is rooted in human nature, which is far more powerful than any organizational issue. As humans, we follow the path of least resistance. If it is easier to associate with people in the church and more difficult with people outside, we will tend to do the easier. Human nature likes cliques. We want to find our place of belonging, our "group," our place of identity, and then camp out there. We don't want to do the work of connecting with people who are not like us. We are comfortable being members together of the enlightened. Cults are only the most extreme form of association and disassociation distinguishing "insiders" and "outsiders," but sectarianism is spread along a spectrum. It is frighteningly easy to get people locked into their church association to the exclusion of other associations. Human nature longs for the safe place. Most people want to be settlers; they don't want to be explorers and pioneers. They will give up good friendships with the unsaved in order to hang out with the saved. The saved love the safe.

A second reason why we withdraw, also rooted in human nature, is that we oftentimes define ourselves by what and whom we are against. A vote for one political candidate is often voting *against* the other person (who surely has horns under his or her hair). Denominations are sometimes the result of more push than pull. Governing regimes in nations know that the best way to get popular support is to focus on an external enemy, real or imagined. So church leaders may consciously or unconsciously emphasize not being "of the world," and neglect the idea of being "in the world" and "sent to the world" (John 17:14–18). Some people applaud sermons that rant and rave about the mean, nasty, ugly world. Church people implore us as leaders to rally them by excoriating our culture and society, not realizing that the way much of this rhetoric comes off to outsiders is as continual whining and posturing as victims. Some churchgoers want us to scold the world for being worldly. And the real tragedy is that it is not for the purpose of doing "the world" any good, but to make themselves feel better.

A third reason we fragment ourselves from the communities we live in is that churches often behave like just one more business establishment along the street, relating to the community in no distinctive way. Municipal authorities a generation ago generally considered churches community assets. Not so in many areas today. Who starts these kinds of territorial skirmishes? It may have been the city board responding to complaints in the neighborhood about traffic congestion and parking issues on Sunday morning. Or it may have been that the church decided on a building program and immediately assumed a truculent stance, pushing its plans on the municipal officials. Once adversarial spirit spoils the air, it is hard for it ever to change. But this doesn't have to be the case.

I remember a time when our church was thinking about moving ten miles west, at an extraordinary cost, giving up a prime location. But we needed a bigger building, and the town board had long let it be known that no building expansion would be allowed. One of our elders in a meeting spoke up: "Someone should go over and talk to the town board. It's an entirely new group of people from what it was a few years ago. Maybe they'd be open to expansion on our own site." That week someone did have a conversation with the town chairman, and to our surprise, the chairman told him to go right ahead and make the request. The door opened at the perfect time. One person, the state highway and roads commissioner, could have been a problem. But when our architect (who also happened to be a member of the church) had a friendly conversation with him, and eased him out of his hesitation with "You don't want to stand in the way of the work of Jesus Christ, do you?" the man relented. But the whole thing was negotiated with mutual respect.

Then there were the neighbors. They were not thrilled about a three-thousand-seat auditorium and related space being built, and they let their objections be known at the town board meeting. But a luncheon meeting for them, at the church, made all the difference. The meeting was an opportunity to get correct information on the table and to let them sound off. As a result, we made some changes in the site layout, committed to using shielding landscaping, and committed to hiring more traffic directors. In the end, the project was approved, the building was doubled, and every year since, the church has kept in close touch with the town board in order to continue to be an asset to the community.

Now this is just one example of a much broader principle. If a church wants to engage with the community, it should see itself as a community asset, and take that posture. When local high schools started asking to hold their commencement ceremony in our auditorium, we were glad to see the building used for a good community event. And they were glad to have access to a comfortable air-conditioned building. That is, except for one or two people several years in a row who objected that a public school commencement in a church building violated the separation of church and state. We always stay neutral, saying that we are happy to let the building be rented, but we aren't pushing for it.

We have no agenda; we are glad if we can be an asset. Each year, an overwhelming vote by graduating families carries the day. Common sense prevails in that the use of a church building does not become the site of a religious battle.

The first decision a church will make about community engagement is whether the church views itself as a part of the community. Not of the world, but definitely being in the world and called to the world.

MORE THAN A THOUSAND POINTS OF LIGHT

Eloquent speechwriter Peggy Noonan came up with a memorable phrase for the inaugural address of George H. W. Bush (the elder Bush) to describe the wonder of on-the-ground community initiatives: "a thousand points of light." Bush used the phrase to describe "a new activism, hands-on and involved," a harnessing of the talent of young and old, a passing on of both leadership and stewardship. He called this movement "a thousand points of light . . . all the community organizations that are spread like stars throughout the Nation, doing good."

I remember having two reactions to "a thousand points of light." First, a positive one. Points of light are a wonderful image of hope. Lighthouses save the lives of ships tossed in storms. The Scripture-copying monks of the dark ages, like candles, helped preserve civilization. Christ-filled believers working in an office can be points of the light of grace and integrity. My second reaction: only *a thousand* community organizations?

In the United States today, there are more than three hundred thousand churches and tens of thousands of other Christian organizations and parachurch ministries. The country is blanketed with believing communities that could live up to Jesus' call for his followers to be salt and light. But oftentimes the light is kept under a bushel, and we make that choice: *Don't want to let the flame blow out; must protect it from the wind. This light, after all, is ours. Outsiders don't "get it."*

And so we dim the light with shades of jargon and cliché, which makes it certain that no one outside the believing community will have access. And churches wonder why outsiders wander in, but leave just as quickly. It would be one thing if they bounced out because no one gave them words they could understand, but if they sensed no grace, that is the real tragedy.

WHAT DOES COMMUNITY ENGAGEMENT LOOK LIKE?

Remember: to engage means *to close the gap between God's resources and human need*. Community engagement means God's people bringing the time, talent, and treasure they have into contact with human need in the community they live in (or nearby, as is the case with many church members I know who have something to offer people living a few communities away). "Volunteerism" will never capture what community engagement is. A person has to volunteer to serve, but when God's resources come into real contact with human need, it is so much more than just helping out. There is a divine power in it.

The great thing about community engagement is that the forms it takes are limited only by our imaginations, which is why one of the most influential things we can do as church leaders is to inspire people's spiritual imaginations. (More about that when we get to the topic of mobilizing people for community engagement.)

Community engagement is missional. People-connection is what makes witness possible. Community engagement is possible through almost any association, service, or function of community life. Last year at the annual congregational meeting at our church, I had thirteen people who are engaged in their communities come up on the platform, and I simply went down the row, microphone in hand, asking them how they were engaging in their community. It struck me how each of them, wide-eyed and enthusiastic, spoke of their connecting point in one of our communities.

Jane, who tutors in music at the rescue mission in the city center. She says she wrote a check supporting this ministry for years, but was transformed when she decided to go and actually do something with the people there.

John, who helps with outreach to Laotian refugees in Milwaukee.

Sharon, who helps at a women's shelter.

Dave, who has volunteered with the Salvation Army for years.

Robin, an engineer, who has received training to be a "marketplace chaplain," ministering to people in the workplace.

Cho, who makes a ministry of befriending international university students.

Janis, who volunteers at a storefront ministry offering health care to disadvantaged city residents.

Jason, who tutors at-risk students in the central city.

Jean, who helps refugees from Myanmar.

Roy, a grey-bearded man in his sixties, who has a ministry to skateboarders. (Yes, that's right, skateboarders.)

Perry, who owns a successful home building company, who leads Bible studies at a residential center for men struggling with drug and alcohol addiction.

Tom, who is a member of the local school board.

Mike, who works at a local food bank.

As I went down the row, microphone in hand, each person was enthusiastic and proud in the best possible way to announce his or her community connection. When people find their point of engagement in their communities, the connection is immensely valuable to them. They know that they have made a commitment to real people. They know that this is the way things are supposed to be—just so commonsense, heaven-inspired, humanly authenticated. And they want others to join in, if not with them in what they do, then with some other form of community engagement.

When we heard those thirteen eager beavers on the platform announce their investment in their community, several things become immediately self-evident:

The possibilities for community engagement are almost endless. We are limited only by our imaginations (but we can easily be hobbled by our hesitations).

Community engagement is for men, women, and children, young and old—it truly cuts across all our distinctions.

It is exciting to have a serving connection with the community.

There is a sense of belonging or identity in having a community connection.

Community engagement gives people a story to tell (actually, many stories of God's grace on the ground).

BEGINNING A MOVEMENT OF COMMUNITY ENGAGEMENT

We could talk a long time about the theory of salt and light, but that has been a problem in the church for centuries: a lot more talk than action. How do we get people *actually* engaged in their communities?

STEP ONE: DISCOVERY

The first step is to find out what community connections people have already made. Community engagement really is a movement of God's Spirit. We should never think that it will start to happen when we make it happen, and certainly never think that community engagement is "accomplished" with one or two great campaigns organized from the top. No matter where your church is, no matter who your members are, no matter whether you've thought actively about community engagement—some people somewhere in your church are already doing it. They may not even be aware that they are bringing together God's resources with human need—they just saw a need, and their instinct was to close the gap. Someone is out there volunteering when a city emergency occurs, serving on a school board, collecting clothing for a resale shop, tutoring disadvantaged students. These people are pioneers, even though they probably don't realize it. Their real-world experience needs to set the pattern for others.

The mustard seed is already in the ground, and it has at least sprouted.

Community engagement is a perfect example of a grassroots movement. And it must be. If your church or mine limited its community connections to the ideas dreamed up by us as leaders, we would be investing in 10 percent of the possible connections, if that. As leaders we have to trust that the ordinary people of God, the troops who are already deployed in the field, will be the first to spot opportunities. And so we should go on a mission of discovery and bring back to the whole congregation a steady stream of incarnational stories.

STEP TWO: ENCOURAGEMENT

When we as leaders discover people who are already investing themselves in community connections, we have a serious responsibility to encourage them—*really* encourage them. It is hard to overstate the power of encouragement when an ordinary person is caught red-handed in an act of grace, and one or more leaders celebrate and encourage that person. When we as leaders do that, we have the privilege and blessing of connecting a person's service in the community with the mission of the church. It is even more powerful when we are encouraging people in doing things we never asked them to do in the first place.

Here is another opportunity for us as leaders to put down our pride and take ourselves out of the spotlight. We are inclined to applaud people who do what we asked them to do because, frankly, it makes *us*, as well as the person acknowledged, look good. But when we encourage people who have served out of their own instincts and imagination and obedience, then we take the focus off of ourselves and our planning. We celebrate one more occasion where God made a move, and a believer stepped up in obedience. And the reason this is important is that if we want to see community engagement become a mighty force in our churches, we have to keep the energy at the grass roots. As soon as we mechanize community engagement, we limit the multiplication.

Encouraging people who have taken the initiative can take many forms:

Send them a note of appreciation.

When you bump into such people, give them a handshake and say, "I heard what you did, and I was so encouraged."

Visit the places where they are serving and let them show you what they are doing.

Briefly tell their story (in a sermon illustration, the church newsletter, at a leaders' meeting) or, better yet, find a time and place where they can tell their story.

Ask them if they would be a reference for other people looking for an avenue of service.

List their community connection when you pull together a list for the wider congregation.

STEP THREE: STORYTELLING

At our church, we recently began a six-month sermon series on the book of Acts, called "Life in the Spirit: What Happens When God Acts." It was a natural step for our fiftieth year as a church because we knew that keeping the focus on God's mighty ways of working was the best way forward into the next decades of ministry. (We also avoided having a fiftieth birthday party for the church because we believed that it is misleading to think of any church as having a specific age. For people who started attending the church two years ago, the church is two years old. There is no such thing as a fifty-year-old church. Any church can have within it the vitality of youth and the stability of the ancient tradition. In fact, every church ought to seek both dynamics.)

The book of Acts is, of course, a running narrative of the acts of the apostles and the acts of God the Holy Spirit. It is story after story of what happens when God acts.

This is a paradigm of local and global witness. How do we train witnesses for Christ, and how do we get them engaged in their communities? We tell the stories. If the stories are told well and the rest of the congregation is challenged to let their imaginations go wild, they will come up with initiatives and connections nobody else would have. We need to challenge people to dream and to take a first step in connecting in their community. It needs to be only a single step. People freeze up when we suggest that we are all looking for that sweeping master strategy. Community engagement will happen much more freely and naturally if people are inspired by the stories and challenged to make just the first step out into new territory.

Robert is a twenty-six-year-old single professional who attends the church's young adult ministry. The weekly large-group meeting, which he attends when he is not traveling on business, is helpful to him. He attended a small group within the ministry for about a year, but never really merged very well with the group.

Two years ago, the young adult ministry decided to make community engagement a significant endeavor of the ministry, and began finding connecting points for its participants. The ministry had a special commitment to a residential center for people with cognitive disabilities, visiting there on Friday nights. In the large-group meeting they told the stories. One week, it was as if a switch were flipped in Robert. He knew he had to find his own connecting point in the community, and he did: tutoring adolescents in math at a center for disadvantaged students.

When we tell the stories of community engagement, many people will take an immediate interest because these are such wonderful "human interest" stories, but then something else goes on, at least in the back of their minds when the imagination takes over.

Drive elderly people to their doctors' appointments? That's something I could do. In fact, I can think of two older people living next door who would be thrilled if I offered to serve them in this way. But . . . maybe I could do more. I love to organize things, and I don't mind making phone calls. I wonder if I could be the one who organizes six drivers to do this ministry?

Telling the stories taps into the compounding effect of different kinds of engagement. A story told in a worship setting becomes a catalyst to singing the next song about purpose and mission; it binds believers to other believers who see more clearly their purpose as a community; and it inspires the imaginations of others who get nudged one step closer to their own community service. Engagement with God, with God's people, and with the community—all working together, exponentially adding energy to each other.

STEP FOUR: ENTRY POINTS

Most churches that are seeing the power of community engagement see the need to develop entry points for people who are not engaged and who do not know where to begin. We need to be prepared to help interested people connect and explore. They need encouragement, and that takes time.

Oftentimes the entry point takes the form of holding organized larger-scale service days.

One church that has developed an extraordinary community engagement ministry is LifeBridge Christian Church in Longmont,

Colorado. Their term for community engagement is "externally focused." For almost two decades, their major focus of ministry has been service in their community.

LifeBridge Christian Church emphasizes two things: tell the stories and give people an entry point. So for years now they have organized two days a year when they mobilize hundreds of people to help out their community in a major one-day effort. The idea is for people who have not discovered service to get a taste of it. And it works.

But it would be a mistake to think that the most important community engagement happens in those one-day projects. Those days are just the spark to light a fire. Some of the most significant community engagement shows up in alliances and partnerships with organizations and agencies in their community. The church provides the people power; the agency provides the venue.

I've named entry points here as step four in a strategy of beginning a movement of community engagement, not because that is where they neatly fit in the chronological order of the steps, but because entry points may not be the place to begin a movement in a church. Discovery is probably a better place to start—especially if it is true that God leads such movements at the grass roots.

James Place is a storefront community outreach in the medium-size city of Waukesha, just west of the location of our church. It is a classic old limestone building along a historic street. Most recently it was an art gallery.

Phil, a member of our church, owns the building. He has a heart for this city. He seems to know practically every businessperson and community leader in the downtown area. One day Phil told our pastor for community engagement that he would be willing to let the building be used for some ministry purpose. The location was great, and the large interior middle room with surrounding side rooms looked very flexible. Using the building seemed to be a no-brainer. Yes.

But there was as yet no ministry organized for it. An outpost waiting for a mission. The building was called the James Building, and someone made the connection with the call of the epistle of James to have faith that works (James 2:17).

It has become a place with multiple functions: there is a parish nurse, supervised by the local hospital, who advises people off the street on resources for their health needs and lifestyle issues; employment counseling; budget counseling; and family movie nights and other recreational activities. It is a place for prayer and Bible study and support groups. Within a year of its beginning, James Place became a hive of activity. Dozens of different ministries occur at this outpost.

And it is this: a field of opportunities where believers can serve. A place where believers will grow in their faith as they learn from the people they are helping. A place to connect people to existing resources in the community. A place to give people dignity by listening to their stories. A way to make a statement to local leaders about the true purpose of Christian faith.

IN PRACTICE—COHESIVE IDEAS FOR A WHOLE CHURCH

---

1. Read *The Externally Focused Church*, by Rick Rusaw and Eric Swanson (Group Publishing, 2004).
2. Discover what the people in your church are already doing in their communities, by speaking on the subject of community engagement and inviting them to e-mail their stories, making sure to define community engagement broadly enough.
3. Discover what community leaders attend your church. Find out how they connect their faith and their work.
4. Start small; esteem small starts so that people get over their hesitation.
5. Study for yourself the biblical idea of community connection and Christian witness.
6. Research the needs of your community by talking to leaders in the business community, education, and government.
7. Look for common ground in working with businesses and other organizations. They may not endorse your efforts in public, but they will value the common work, and may tell you that in private.
8. Begin to teach the value of community engagement to all leaders in the church.

9. Have a conversation with anyone you discover who is serving in the community. Send a note of encouragement or make a phone call.

10. Encourage these people by asking them periodically how their work is going.

11. Begin to tell the stories early. Don't wait for a change of philosophy of ministry in your church. The stories of divine supply connecting with human need will make the case.

12. Learn about any other churches in your community that are connecting well with the community. Find out how they are doing it.

13. Encourage people to think in concentric circles of influence. The community one person may serve is his or her neighborhood; for another it is forty-five minutes away.

14. Look for community engagement opportunities that cross over racial or ethnic lines.

15. Inspire the young adults in the congregation who are looking for a fresh sense of mission.

16. Avoid making community engagement a program. A group does not need matching shirts to form a team that will do community work. And don't make it about giving away money. The real value is in relationships.

17. Ask leaders of parachurch ministries in your community how they might use more volunteers.

18. Look for openings that will make a long-term difference in people's lives: assistance to kids at risk or to teens at risk. Be bold; try something new; be creative.

19. Take a few months to properly plan a large-scale community service day. Make it a rallying point for the church.

20. Do not use the large-scale service day as a litmus test for what might happen in the future. You may feel enthusiastic or discouraged the first time you try an event like this.

21. Over time, recruit key leaders who organize and—most important—guide and encourage whole teams of volunteers. Follow through!

22. More and more often, tell the stories of community engagement through, for instance, testimonial in worship service, stories in print in the church newsletter, or videos posted on the church Web site.

23. Keep in touch with local government leaders. Don't come at them with missionary zeal. Meet them; show an interest in the community.
24. Ask community leaders this key question: Where are the gaps in what you are having to do for people? This specific question will open doors because community leaders are well aware of their gaps.
25. Find one such gap and begin there.

7

ENGAGE WITH THE WORLD

A WHOLE CHURCH FOR THE WHOLE WORLD

THE BIG IDEA
There is greatness in the ideal of the Whole Church because of the greatness of God's grace and the greatness of the mission given to the body of Christ. One of the best antidotes to small-mindedness in the church, and one of the best ways for us to believe in the Whole Church, is to lead people into a personal connection with the worldwide Christian movement.

Every Christmas, I love to ponder the words of the Magnificat, the Virgin Mary's song following the visitation of the angel Gabriel, which begins with this explosive expression:
My soul magnifies the Lord.
I like to speak on this passage because you see people fascinated by this simple proposition: Mary did not magnify the Lord in the sense of making God bigger. Rather, her soul at that moment apprehended a greater vision of who God is, and that larger vision gave her a greater heart, poured out in that great song.
That is what happens to believers when they receive a vision of the expansive and remarkable work of God's Spirit all over the world.

When I was a nerdy sixth grader captivated by space technology and astronomy, I remember going out the first time with a telescope, pointing it at the moon—and being knocked back by the vastly larger image of this presence in the sky. I could see that the moon was a real place with mountains and plains and ravines, and in an instant it ceased being just a white disk in the evening sky.

All of us are candidates for a larger vision.

The churches I grew up in were not big on global mission, but when I was in college I began to hear the stories—told by missionaries and international travelers—of the one great God doing extraordinary things in the most alien and exotic places. I experienced an epiphany. Without traveling ten miles from home, I began to "travel" the world, because the very best storytellers could truly take you places.

There were, of course, many missionaries who were not at all skilled in using words to describe their experiences, and the slides in their presentations were often at the wrong exposure ("Now this slide shows . . . or it would show if it weren't underexposed . . ."). And there were a few storytellers who had obviously embellished their stories a bit for effect, which didn't seem to me to be consistent with the gospel of truth. But I nonetheless gained something from their enthusiasm if nothing else.

We live in a different time now. Perfectly exposed digital pictures and even well-edited video assists the storyteller. Maybe it's a bit harder to embellish stories when there's video evidence. But these communication tools make it possible for us to take this further step in maturity: today we are all doing more work *interpreting* the world, not just observing it from a distance. And what a world it is! Despite the efforts of the atheist crusaders, we see a world that is not any less religious today. Human beings across cultures and national boundaries still show this irrepressible drive to connect with their Creator. But with more detailed knowledge of the world, we know we need to wrestle with the undercurrents of religious extremism that are like a hidden riptide ready to carry people out to oblivion. We get much more information about the clash of Hindus and Muslims in the Far East. The news conveys stories of extremist Hindu persecutions of Christians in northern and eastern India. We hear the amazing story of the spread of Christianity in China. We wonder how to interpret it all. And when we

are wisest, we know we can't settle for parochialism. We know we
need to engage with the world.

TWENTY PEOPLE, SEVENTEEN
COUNTRIES, THREE WEEKS

Engaging with the world means engaging with people. World mission is not an abstraction, not a motto, not a philosophy. World
mission happens when engagement happens—when God's supply
is brought into contact with human need. And that sometimes happens with a personal introduction across national boundaries.

It was a Wednesday afternoon, and twenty of us were sitting
on chairs in a circle in a conference room at a retreat center
in Milwaukee, snacks and drinks aplenty on tables at the back.
Twenty people, representing seventeen different countries. These
church leaders had traveled from around the world at our invitation, to be together for three weeks. The concept of the International Center is simple: gather a reasonable-size group of church
leaders from all over the world, give them two-and-a-half weeks
together (three weeks including travel), let the agenda of discussion rise out of their interests and needs—but most important,
base the whole "learning community" experience on a personal
bond they gain with each other. On Wednesday, all of us, many
with jet lag, had just met. By Saturday we were friends. Troy, a pastor from Bermuda, told me that if he went home after three days,
the gathering would have been worth the effort.

As we did for other sessions of the International Center, we
invited participants on the basis of recommendations by people
we know who have connections overseas. We pray that God will
orchestrate it all, combining experienced leaders with younger
leaders, different denominations, different cultures. Participants
have included Jean-Marie, a pastor from Burundi; Rudy, a children's ministry leader (and former army drill sergeant!) from
South Africa, with an unforgettable clipped accent and a forceful
personality; Iwonka and Tomak, two recently wed church planters from a small city in Poland; Mipo, the president of the largest Protestant denomination in West Africa, with five thousand

churches under his care; Michael, a young pastor from the Czech Republic; Roberto, from Brazil; Thespal, a pastor from a city in northern India; Ram, a pastor from Nepal. That's just half the group. Take a group photo of these folks, and you'll have a most amazing display of clothing, color, and personal style. They make each other smile.

The agenda for the first three days at the retreat center is simple—each person is given half an hour to tell the group about his or her background, growing up, family, spiritual life, and ministry, and then about twenty minutes for follow-up questions from the group. Participants all want the others to know about their families, especially, and their conversion or calling. After a day, the members start to talk about how startling they find this gathering. They expected to come to the United States and take notes from a series of lecturers. They didn't expect anyone to ask them about themselves. Some say they've *never* been asked about themselves. They didn't think that *they* would be the agenda. We pray for these leaders after they share. There are three leaders from Myanmar at this session, and they got out of the country just before a revolution started. We pray every day for their families and their country. At break time, conversation is lively.

Laughter comes easily right from the start—the Africans always help with that. And there are plenty of throat-choking stories: Alan from Rwanda, who is clearly still deeply traumatized by the carnage he witnessed firsthand; Larissa from Tajikistan, who has lived with hardship and the death of her husband and children; Anna from Nepal, who has seen the darkness of false gods; Hubert, a physician and World Relief head from Haiti whose stories of voodoo in action will make the hair stand up on the back of your neck. You won't get all that if you don't take the time. And when their stories are all through, each person knows he or she has taken a risk, has offered a piece of himself or herself to a group of strangers who are true brothers and sisters of the Whole Church.

The pattern for each day of the remaining two weeks includes morning devotions and a topic of discussion for the morning, usually facilitated by members of our church's staff: ministry to men, women, children; poverty; globalization; small group ministry; evangelism and apologetics; HIV-AIDS, and so on. After lunch is free time for participants to do what is best for them: rest, hold ad hoc gatherings, study, hold an extra session. Evenings are for ministry visitation. Weekends are spent with their host families or in a cultural experience, such as going to a Milwaukee Brewers baseball game. Twenty people, seventeen countries, sitting in the stands asking every conceivable question about the unusual game on the field, which to them seems painfully slow.

They sit together in the worship service of the church and are warmly applauded when introduced. To our congregation in that moment they represent the world, and we remind ourselves of what happens with mustard seeds well planted.

At the banquet on the last day together, the guests of the International Center share their insights. What we hear is astonishing. They have been each other's teachers. The truths learned are incarnate in the lives of these leaders and in the vivid cultures they represent. We all have learned again that the gifts of God's Spirit are indeed distributed throughout the whole body of Christ, the Whole Church. We have invested real time and thought and concern.

Every leader goes back home with a different paradigm of training, and an optimism that fragmentation and bias can at least be lessened if we are each other's teachers. It is not that the American church is God's gift to the world—the Whole Church is. These people go back home with new alliances that none of them would have imagined: a church in Belfast now partnered with a work in India, a South African link with Rwanda, and Tajikistan has forged a connection with Poland. Only God knows what will lead to what. When a monsoon decimated Myanmar last year, we were able to help a Bible college because of our knowledge of and relationship with the principal, who was a participant at the International Center. When a tsunami destroyed whole regions of Indonesia and India, our link with Paul in India gave us an opportunity to provide direct and immediate assistance.

We say we believe in the Whole Church. But this reality becomes concrete when the gap is closed, and we take the time to look in the faces of brothers and sisters who live many time zones away. But even if we can't be in the same room, there are ways for any church to come face-to-face with the Whole Church.

ENGAGING WITH THE WORLD—AN ORGANIC REALITY FOR EVERY CHRIST-FOLLOWER

Followers of Christ already have the most important equipment for engaging with the world. It isn't a plane, cable TV, or the Internet— it is the soul. When Christ truly liberates someone, his or her spirit is freed from narcissism and parochialism. When a person finds the Savior for all time, Christ Pantocrator ("Ruler of all," so powerfully depicted in Eastern Christian art), that person has joined a larger world. The family of God includes members who come from truly every part of the world today. A believing Christian lives in a house-hold with a thousand languages but one idiom.

This is not just rhetoric. It is reality. A Christ-follower has to have a global perspective, not because it is the educated thing to do or the politically correct thing to do, but because it simply is reality. I have no earthly explanation for how I can travel to a country in a faraway place (say China or Ethiopia or Romania), meet there people I have never seen before, and, literally within minutes, experience with them the bond of brother and sister in Christ. Revelation's vision of people from every tribe, language, people, and nation worshiping Christ is not just apocalyptic—it is happening now. But most people in our churches will not go to an international congress on world mission. They may never stand in one room with dozens of nationalities praising God at the same time. We need to help bring the world to them, and it is possible for any church of any size anywhere to do so.

PARADIGM SHIFT—HOW THE WORLD GAP HAS BEEN CLOSING

We've been told many times how television, cable news, radio, the Internet, and other media are rapidly closing the world gap. Thomas Friedman's *The World Is Flat* demonstrates how world economies are linking nationalities through commercial interest. And I am still amazed at the ease with which many young adults in their twenties go globe-trotting. The incredible shrinking world does put us in a different cultural milieu than that of our parents and grandparents, but the question is, What will we do with the opportunities that global communications and travel afford us? How will we interpret the world? And how will we reach out across cultures?

In the past, a church's involvement on the global scene may have been limited to writing checks out of a missions budget to help support cross-cultural missionaries. The engagement with the world increased exponentially when that church made a personal connection with those missionaries: linking a small group with a missionary for prayer and other support, giving a missionary quality exposure to the church when visiting, holding an annual missions festival, and so on.

I still consider some of the intrepid missionaries I have known for decades as one of the best means I have to understand the wider world, and a true inspiration to me of commitment to the cause. When I travel overseas, I am at a location for mere days or weeks; these people are planted in their places of work and can offer true understanding. There are still areas of the world where there is no substitute for a missionary willing to go for years at a time and engaging in evangelism, training, relief work, or whatever the calling is. But other opportunities are opening up as well.

One paradigm shift that opens the possibilities for global engagement is the forging of direct connections between churches and overseas works. Whereas churches in the past had always depended on agencies as the necessary middleman in supporting work overseas, now churches are starting to form direct relationships with Christian works and workers in compelling and strategic parts of the world.

The Congo Initiative is the vision of Dr. David Kasali, who returned to his homeland after being the principal of one of Africa's premier theological seminaries. In a war-ravaged country with hardly any infrastructure, David and his wife and other dedicated workers have founded a university, a center for family development, a church development center, and another center for the arts. It is a place of hope in a land of hopelessness. And it has been a perfect opportunity for our church to partner with good friends on the ground.

Relationships with the leaders of Asian Outreach have made this organization a viable strategic initiative connection. Asian Outreach trains tens of thousands of church planters, treat hundreds of thousands at medical clinics, help poverty-stricken people in China through microenterprise loans to women. With 64 percent of the world's population, Asia is not just some of the world; it is most of the world. There is no way a church can be a Whole Church without attempting to connect with the church in Asia.

For eighteen years, Elmbrook supported church planters in Romania (before and after the fall of communism) by supporting Tom and Mary as key missionaries. Tom and his family are back in the states now, and he serves as missions pastor, but the engagement with Romania continues now through a direct support of a program of leadership training.

It is likely that the years to come will see ever-increasing numbers of churches seeking direct relationships with Christian works overseas. When the right partnerships are formed (which involves a lot more than just agreeing to write checks to the most effective fundraisers), a church has an opportunity for long-term mutual encouragement and personal involvement.

Engaging with the world means engaging with people.

We are not limited to any one method of engaging with the world. Much of it has to do with telling the stories—not a new idea. We know Jesus through the narrative of the Gospels. We understand how the Spirit of God works through the stories of the book of Acts. Any church can start today, or grow today, in engagement with the world by bringing the story home. And then asking God for a call to do something.

- -
IN PRACTICE—COHESIVE IDEAS
FOR A WHOLE CHURCH
- -

1. As a leader, develop your own convictions about the world Christian movement through a fresh reading of Scripture, prayer, and educating yourself on the latest developments in world mission.
2. Lead members of the church into a substantial prayer connection with the world. Make links with international workers or works.
3. Invite people to join in focus groups that adopt a country, a region of the world, or a global issue that they can learn

about, pray for, and be advocates for (for instance: China, East Africa, Germany, Israel, India, Romania, Gulf Coast, HIV-AIDS, friends of internationals, and so on).

4. In sermons, intentionally use illustrations from the wider world.
5. Teach about the world Christian movement, but be vivid and concrete.
6. Host international guests.
7. Sponsor some kind of annual "mission festival" or "world festival"; invite a special speaker who can inform about God's work in the world and inspire others.
8. Have an international dinner with excellent ethnic foods. It is amazing how food can become the catalyst for talking about the wider world and God's activity in it.
9. Make a special fund in the church's budget for global outreach, using, for instance, the mechanism of "faith promise" (that is, an annual confidential promise, made by faith by members of a church, that collectively becomes the world outreach budget for the year; faith promise generates much enthusiasm and commitment in many churches).[1]
10. Make alliances with global partners.
11. Support overseas missionaries, but connect with them at a personal level.
12. Support short-term mission efforts that are truly fruitful (a trip to Mexico for high schoolers; a building project for a Native American community; a trip to a church in Africa to train Christian educators). The possibilities are endless, but they need to be carefully planned and teams carefully trained. An ill-conceived trip can be a gigantic waste of time and resources, whereas a fruitful trip can result in changed values and a life-long commitment to mission by people on the trip.
13. Do something, even if it seems modest, when there is news of devastation in some part of the world. Organizations like World Relief exist to link churches with world need.
14. Correct people when they want to separate evangelism from social action. This is easily done with the teachings of Jesus and the great history of world mission.
15. Seed small groups amply with prayer ideas and requests from the wider world.

16. Set up a method for a small group to adopt a country or a missionary or international worker.

17. Tell the story—of something you learned about the worldwide Christian movement.

18. Tell the story—by communicating testimonials from believers who are being transformed by their experiences in global engagement.

19. Tell the story—by praying for a part of the world when it is devastated by a natural catastrophe.

20. Tell the story—by letting a visiting missionary speak directly to the congregation.

21. Tell the story—by placing an international phone call during the worship service (or playing a prerecorded conversation) with an international worker. (This is very effective when some catastrophe has hit.)

22. Tell the story—by using graphics and other visuals when speaking about other parts of the world.

23. Tell the story—by showing a video prepared by an international worker.

24. Tell the story—of anybody in the church who has been a refugee sponsor.

25. Challenge, challenge, challenge. Keep the Great Commission front and center. Give people hope for themselves by leading them into a world much bigger than themselves.

PART THREE

THE DYNAMICS OF THE WHOLE CHURCH

8

THE DYNAMICS OF COHESION

THE BIG IDEA
Unity should be a core reality in a church, but it takes many different cohesive experiences to work against the dynamics of fragmentation.

Whenever a church is going through a significant transition—of leadership, of strategy, of philosophy—there are two dynamics that will help the transition succeed: cohesion and momentum. *Cohesion is the set of forces that hold a church together; momentum is the action and forward motion that gives a congregation a sense of purpose.* We'll look at the dynamics of cohesion in this chapter and those of momentum in the next.

Here is a dangerous thought for the day: stop and think about how effective the ministry of our churches would be if, instead of fractiousness and division, we lived and modeled true unity. It's a dangerous thought because it could quickly take us to discouragement and despondency. We know that our churches, and practically all churches, and for all time have often languished in disunity. In the annals of shame of divisive church history we can include

The church in Corinth that could not figure out what to do with open sexual immorality and had a raging battle of the sexes going on, and whose gatherings sometimes did more harm than good

The church in Ephesus that let love melt away

The churches of North Africa in the fourth century that became divided because of an exaggerated puritanical attitude (these churches, divided down the middle, ended up weakened prior to the sweep of Islam across the region)

The cultural divisions between the practical Westerners and the philosophical Easterners, resulting in the Great Schism of 1054

The push and pull between clergy and laity, bishops and princes, orders and hierarchy during the Middle Ages

The inability of the early Protestant churches to be united in their efforts to reform

The multiplication of church splits and acrimonious subdividing of denominations

And you know the list could go on. Our history is what it is. The question is whether we can forge a different path forward in the future. The answer to the question is yes, but only if we *choose* a different path. And we will choose unity only if we *cherish* it.

I know that early in my ministry I valued unity. How could anyone not? And, after all, the Bible says we're supposed to be unified in the church. But with the passage of time, I realized that it is not enough just to give a nod to unity or even to insist on it. We have to love it. We have to be out-of-our-minds enthusiastic when we see the miracle of "neither Jew nor Gentile, male nor female, slave nor free." When a church comes together for a common cause, we need to celebrate it as warriors celebrate the victory at the end of a great battle, because it is a victory against dark powers whose tactics include destruction through fragmentation.

And this is key: when our churches show authentic unity, that unity includes the respectful inclusion of dissenting voices. Unity is not the same thing as uniformity. Unity is living as a body with members who are different from each other. Although it is popular to speak about the value of diversity in society, the church's call is to recognize the genius of God in diversity. In the church, we don't merely admire diversity as one is impressed by the different colors of the rainbow, but we are awed at how God has crafted the human race to be a dynamic collaboration. This is God's way, and it is God's will.

In this chapter, we are going to talk about unity not as theory but as practice, and we will focus on unity at the level of the congregation. Our biblical charge is this: "Make every effort to keep the unity of the Spirit through the bond of peace" (Eph. 4:3). In any given week I can ask myself, *Have I made "every effort to keep the unity of the Spirit"?* And the honest answer has to be no. I may have made some effort, I may even have made an exerted effort, but I can rarely say that I have made "every effort." The fact that the apostle Paul would have to say "make every effort" tells us that unity is never won by a nod of the head and certainly not with a casual acquiescence to the principle of unity. We have to cherish it enough that we will expend every effort, give up every shred of self-interest, and redefine our measure of "success" on the basis of God's shout for unity. We have to give up the image of the solitary leader reaching the summit of an icy mountain peak, and instead embrace the image of a liberating army sweeping through a war-ravaged town.

COHESION

In high school physics class, we are taught about cohesion and adhesion. Cohesion is the sticking together of particles of the same substance, whereas adhesion is the sticking together of particles of different substances. So when you use a piece of Scotch tape to stick a piece of paper on a window, that is *adhesion* (and why it is called, generically, adhesive tape). But when you spill water on a table and see it bead up or gather in pools, you are witnessing *cohesion*. (This actually occurs at the molecular level, because the hydrogen and oxygen molecular structure is highly attractive.)

So how is your week going as a church leader? Do you feel as though you're running around frantically putting adhesive tape on relationships and organizational details in order to hold them together? Or do you feel as though you put people in a room (a worship center, a committee room) and they just come together like water beading on a table, because their attraction to each other is so strong?

Leaders who try to make people adhere to each other live in continual frustration. Leaders who seek unity based on the power of spiritual cohesion in Christ at least have a chance. The question is, what can we as church leaders do to promote cohesion?

There are two ways of achieving unity in a church. One is to appeal to the principle of unity as the spiritual reality of the body of Christ; the other is to promote experiences of cohesion—dozens of experiences, hundreds of experiences. Some leaders naturally do the first—appealing to unity; others produce unity through actions that pull people together. The truth is that we need both. Like the pooling of water in the physical world that happens at the molecular level, the essential attraction that is our bond in Jesus Christ must be the basis of unity, and to experience it we need to bring people together in bonding experiences.

APPEALING FOR UNITY

We'll move on to the practicalities of cohesive experiences shortly, but first we should ask how church leaders can lead people (and lead themselves) away from our baser instincts of ego and separation and toward the ideal of unity. When we appeal for unity, how can we make sure it is not just rhetoric?

Just using the word "ideal" is risky because it means not only "one's conception of what is perfect or most suitable" but also "existing only in the imagination." If someone calls you an idealist, do you take it as a compliment or as an insult? Is idealism high-mindedness or naive dreaminess? Church leaders know that unity is an ideal—but is it realistic or just wishful thinking?

If there is any place where ideals should be and can be real, it is the church.

I'm reminded of the oft-quoted Rodney King, the African American man whose videotaped beating by Los Angeles police back in 1991 was a catalyst for race riots that left fifty-three dead, thousands injured, and seven thousand fires set. At the height of the violence days after the incident, King made a statement to the television cameras and microphones that became immediately memorable: "Can we all get along?" It was a plaintive cry, made by a man whose bruised face was the real message of the appeal. That no one in public life really answered the question implied that the answer to "Can we all get along?" was either "Good question" or "Probably not."

If you have been leading in the church long enough, you have asked yourself the question "Can we all get along?" But there's a pretty good chance that if you ever posed that question in front of a congregation, you would be met with silence. Believers know in their hearts that yes, we should be able to get along, but why is it that when we talk about unity it just seems like rhetoric? It goes in one ear and out the other. Is it because our appeal to unity oftentimes doesn't get past pleading—a Rodney King–type appeal in the middle of wreckage?

The appeal for unity has to have the power of God in it; otherwise there is not a chance for cohesion. "Make every effort to keep the unity of the Spirit through the bond of peace." This is the key: it is the unity *of the Spirit*—the kind of unity that happened on the day of Pentecost when thousands of people from different countries all visiting Jerusalem during the festival were drawn together when the Spirit was "poured out" (no intentional allusion to the water analogy I used earlier—but maybe there should be). Pentecost was people coming together to celebrate God's liberating grace (the symbolism of the Feast of Weeks), but they were bonded together when God's Spirit moved across them. Engagement between people was fully realized as the consequence of their powerful engagement with God. There is an analogy to our lives today. We gather people for worship, and that's a good and powerful sign, but we can go through the motions and everyone separates, unchanged, unless the worship is an act of the Spirit on us. But what does that mean? Everyone wants to know what worship "in the Spirit" means. One main interpretation takes the words to mean "in the realm of the Spirit." Worship in the Spirit is not measured by any particular activities (such as supernatural occurrences), but rather is found when our worship launches beyond the physical, beyond the ritual, and beyond the human. Worship in the Spirit happens when we get beyond ourselves, far beyond ourselves—when we know that we are listening for the voice of God. You can't measure that by volume or verve. The Spirit moves as the Spirit chooses, sometimes imperceptibly. One of the ways we know that we have gotten beyond the physical and beyond the ritual, that we have been made to "drink of one Spirit," is that we see a unity of the Spirit. When worshipers believe that they have shared a common grace of God the Spirit, they walk away with a sense of being bound together.

And as long as we're talking about worship in the Spirit, we should remember that Jesus said that true worshipers worship "in Spirit *and in truth.*" There are a hundred different reasons why we should make every effort to impart truth in our worship. One of them is to promote unity. Give people a truth-filled worship experience, and they will walk away more unified. Provide them with a pattern of weekly truth-filled worship, and the weight of the truth will be a centripetal force pulling people toward the center of that truth. The preaching-teaching-proclamation ministry of the church will always be one of the most powerful forces in promoting a Whole Church.

A message or sermon is the primary means we'll think of, but beyond that, truth telling and truth celebrating can come through a revealing personal story or testimony, through well-spoken prayers, and even through the serious and careful recitation of Scripture. People are so hungry for truth as the bedrock reality they can count on that when they find truth in worship—throughout the worship—they are bound to each other without even thinking about it. They are like people running to a shelter when tornado sirens are sounding all around. They're grateful to find the shelter, and only afterwards do they realize that they have gathered into a community with others who likewise have heard the alarm and came together under the secure shelter of the truth.

One kind of engagement multiplies another. A true engagement with God in worship brings about a true engagement of God's people with each other. In other words, unity is the by-product of true engagement. When churches try to achieve unity by force of will, it is though they were attempting to build a house with adhesive tape. When, instead, the power of unity is a force acting upon a congregation, then that force is truly capable of forming a bond. And the force is God the Spirit.

Are there times to appeal for unity for the sake of unity? Yes, but only if we understand that the principle goes beyond "let's all just get along."

EXPERIENCES OF COHESION

Like many church leaders, as my appreciation for the importance of church unity grew, I thought that what I needed to do was to remind people at every possible opportunity of the importance of unity. But then I noticed two things: first, mere talk about unity can quickly take the tone of catchphrase—something you give a nod to (how can you not agree with the principle of unity?), but it doesn't translate into real-life terms in people's minds. The other thing I noticed is that it was the real experiences of cohesion—when we came through experiences of solidarity and connection that we became enthusiastic about—that had the greatest effect in unifying a congregation. Engagement is its own best argument.

What I mean by "experiences of cohesion" are those moments when in some large or small way, people are bound to each other, and they come out the other side realizing how right the bond is. We most powerfully authenticate the message of reconciliation (which means being pulled together across a divide) when we actually experience being together for a right cause.

Most churches have experiences of cohesion whether they are conscious of them or not. But we must be conscious of them because cumulative cohesive experiences help us to be Whole Churches. We must sustain a commitment to having cohesive experiences in every dimension. To have them throughout the year. To keep creating new ones. A garment isn't held together by a few irregular stitches, but by long lines of carefully placed ones.

Here, then, are types of cohesive experiences, with some examples.

THE TEACHABLE MOMENT

There are always events and trends in society that are opportunities to apply the gospel, but what we should really watch for are those moments when the whole of our community's eyes are captivated by one thing. These are teachable moments. When, in 1990, it was obvious that the United States was going to go to war to liberate Kuwait from the army of Saddam Hussein, my colleagues and I sensed that it was a teachable moment to learn about a Christian worldview and the gospel. So over four successive Sunday nights we had public lectures: "A Christian View of War," "Iraq and the Bible," "Why Bad Things Happen," and "Prophecy and Current Events." By design they were not sermons but instead lectures by two of us on our staff and two guest speakers, offering the audience much detailed information and research. I remember people hanging on every word, not just because these were interesting topics but because they were timely and expedient. What I most remember are the comments from people who said that they were so proud that their church opened up important questions and was offering substantive answers at a critical time. Everyone knew that in this post–Cold War era, we were about to enter a new time of high-tech warfare in a part of the world that was a tinderbox. Here's the point: everyone in our community and nation was sitting on the edge of his or her seat because of the likelihood of an impending war. It was a teachable moment in which to draw people together. Not to do so would have meant that the church was acting like an ostrich with its head in the sand. (I remember hearing from someone about a church in Dallas that did not even mention the assassination of President Kennedy the Sunday after it happened—as if the church were too much above "the world" to bother itself with its messes. Wow.) Our people don't just want us to speak; they want us to speak *into* their lives and *into* the changing circumstances of life.

Another teachable moment was when the country's attention was riveted on a sex scandal in the White House in 1997 and beyond. The president of the United States had admitted to an inappropriate relationship with a White House intern. He was caught, and he apologized to the country. The whole issue of guilt and forgiveness was put on the national agenda. So we offered a Sunday night lecture on the subject: "Should the President Be Forgiven?" The purpose was to use the occasion as a kind of test case for what biblical theology has to say about forgiveness for all of us—what really is forgiveness, and what are its limits? It was a cohesive experience because national events put an essential life issue, forgiveness, front and center in people's minds.

Sometimes a teachable moment is not something taking place at the national level, but instead is a local phenomenon. For every citizen of the state of Wisconsin (except for the occasional renegade), devotion to the Green Bay Packers comes naturally. It is not just the legend of the team led by Lombardi, but the fact that the small city of Green Bay (population of about a hundred thousand—where I grew up with great enthusiasm!) is always a David challenging the Goliaths around. So in 1996–97, when the Packers marched triumphantly through a season that everyone saw as their destiny year, and on into the Super Bowl, it seemed as though something special was called for on that Sunday. So for my message that weekend, I chose "How to Have a Super Life" (well illustrated, of course, by some of my recollections of growing up in Green Bay). It is not that we were obligated to do something different that weekend, and it certainly wasn't that the agenda of the church was hijacked by a sport event. It simply was a teachable moment too juicy to pass up. The whole community was enthusiastic during that football season beyond anything I remember. The euphoria was building for many weeks. The Packers were, at that moment, a force of cohesion in the community. Everybody was looking in the same direction. So why not use that teachable moment to apply the gospel? Why not take a common vision and raise it to a higher level, even giving meaning to the experience of joy? It wasn't hard at all to come up with a gospel message: If the Super Bowl for the home team is this exciting, how much more is the prospect of living—by the grace of God—a super life? Hebrews 12 provided the principles.

The teachable moment is a cohesive moment because when everyone's ears are turned in the same direction, and the church offers a credible voice, people will learn again that the gospel really does bring life together, and not just at times of social crises but in the good times as well.

A HISTORIC TURNING POINT

All churches have anniversaries and other occasions that are turning points. These are times when a church looks backward and forward at the same time. They are portals or doorways. The Roman god Janus, depicted as a bearded figure with two faces pointed in opposite directions, was the god of gates and doorways and new beginnings. The month of January is named for this god of beginnings.

Churches sometimes let "January moments," the historic turning points, slip by. Or they celebrate an anniversary without looking with vision to the future. Nostalgia may produce gratitude, but it must be joined to vision in order for us to march into the future.

In the past decade, our church has passed its fortieth and fiftieth anniversaries. Both were significant milestones, but we might have let both of them pass us by if we had planned mere birthday celebrations or moments of nostalgia.

As we approached our fortieth anniversary in 1998, some suggested that spiritual renewal in the church could be the order of the day, and they were certainly right. Someone suggested forty nights of prayer, and it happened. In our chapel, about 150 to 200 people gathered every evening during that period to pray. Someone else suggested a forty-day spiritual growth emphasis, so we wrote and provided a forty-day devotional called *A Forty-Day Journey with God.* There was, of course, a celebration weekend, but it focused as much on the future as on the past. What none of us knew at the time was that we would be facing some of our greatest challenges as a church in the following five years. I am convinced that the cohesion of our church during the historic turning point of our fortieth anniversary gave us the strength and stability to meet those challenges.

The year before our fiftieth anniversary, we decided to explore the theme of Jubilee in the Old Testament. On a one-day retreat of our pastoral staff, we studied the biblical theme, exploring what it may mean for us. We knew immediately that this was to be God's movement at this time for us. It was just too good to pass up. In the Old Testament, Jubilee is a kind of super-sabbath, a year of giving the land a rest, of forgiving debt, of allowing displaced people sold into indentured servitude to be released from their slavery. Jesus began his ministry by saying that the promises of "the acceptable year of the Lord" were about to be fulfilled in him. Everything would be different.

Our church began a "year of Jubilee" with a fifty-day period of learning seven great Jubilee truths: sabbath, redemption, freedom, forgiveness, healing, justice, proclamation. Seven weekend worship services, fifty days of devotions for adults, teens, and children. Lots of storytelling. But the focus was as much on the present and the future as it was on the past.[1]

There is an important difference between *historical* and *historic.* A historical event merely means "occurring in history," but a historic event is a momentous happening that has significance for the future. When a church merely floats through an anniversary on the river of time, marking the historical passage, it makes little difference in the life of the church. Marking a historical moment may produce nostalgia, some good memories, and a sense of celebration, but a year later what remains is the spiritual scrapbook.

But to make something a historic moment is to define the future, not just the past.

One person (a key leader) who had been attending our church for a few years told me that the fortieth anniversary celebration was nice, but that she had never felt more like an outsider, as all these stories were told of a past generation. We determined that our fiftieth year, the year of Jubilee, would mark lessons from the past, but would quickly move to the present and the future.

A fiftieth celebration is historic. But for many churches, a twentieth anniversary or even a tenth can be interpreted as a historic turning point. Even a first-year anniversary of a brand-new church is historic. One trip around the sun, one cycle through the seasons. Historic turning points are opportunities for cohesion. They are not merely birthdays, but birth days of future new life.

IMPARTING A VISION

Although there is little debate anymore about the importance of vision in the church, we often have a very limited view of what vision is. We need a clearer vision of vision. Some portray vision as big, splashy, bold ideas. The more outrageous the better. The pricier the better. And although there are times when churches need to launch out on daring initiatives, the vision of a church is much broader than that.

We shouldn't complicate this. Vision means *seeing*. When a church's leaders keep their spiritual eyes open and continuously scan for the gifts and graces of God, that is vision. It is seeing the potential for leadership in that young person who doesn't see it in himself or herself. It is noticing a sliver of a crack of an opportunity to bring light into the community by starting a new downtown ministry.

Sometimes vision is a bold faith-stretching project, such as relocating the church or building a new facility. Almost always our dreams will stretch our resources. If the idea is sound and the people have a sense of ownership in it, the project can be realized. But the people need to be given a vision for it. They need their eyes to be pointed at something that does not yet exist. Vision is Spirit-inspired imagination and Spirit-directed motivation. And so it is not limited to building projects and budgets. Vision as the ordinary experience of a church means seeing the spiritual movements afoot in a church and seeing what spiritual movements are possible.

Vision is a powerful cohesive force in a church. Get people looking in the same direction and moving down the road together, and that will help hold them together (more about that in the next chapter on momentum). But the solitary leader must not assume that his or her vision does pull people together. What if a leader's vision springs from personal ambition or arbitrary whim? Sometimes dreams are vision; sometimes they are fantasy. A vision is not authenticated by how colorful or flashy it is. Vision can mean seeing possibilities far down the road, but most of the time vision means seeing the next steps ahead. If you're driving to the Rocky Mountains, you can keep the mountain range in your vision, but you also have to keep your eyes on the road.

Even in the case of a good vision, it may not be a cohesive force until people gain the sense of vision for themselves. Leaders must wait and see what happens in the people as they live with a vision for a while. There are no guarantees that most of the people will see it, but at least some of them must. For vision to be a cohesive force, it must be authenticated by a group of leaders who can test the original idea.

RESPONDING TO A CRISIS

Ironically, sometimes a crisis that could fragment a church becomes an opportunity for cohesion—but only if the church rises to the occasion. In the far too common experience of the moral failure of church leaders, churches often hemorrhage members because of people's sense of betrayal or simple discouragement. But it is amazing how many churches survive and even grow through the experience. There is nothing like failure to demolish self-righteousness or a puritanical disposition in a church. Biblical theology tells us that human nature is fragile and fractured, but that God is unalterably great and good and provides power and grace to protect us from our failures. So even the fragmenting experience of a crisis can be a rallying point and a time to pull together.

A natural disaster in a community often produces a strong sense of community connection as people pull together to respond to the crisis. Churches may be the best rapid-response organizations that exist. If something disastrous happens in a community, churches have an immediate opportunity to act on the instincts of grace and generosity and spring into action, delivering food and blankets, offering shelter, providing spiritual comfort and trauma counseling—whatever the essential needs of the moment may be.

The churches were places of refuge in Columbine, Colorado, after two students shot and killed twelve of their classmates and one teacher in an episode of dark rage. Prayer meetings, counseling sessions, worship services, funerals—all were powerful engagement events. God's grace coming together with human need. People engaged with other people. Their point of connection was the gap in their souls created by the wounding of evil, and the instinct to find truth and love to fill the gap. And people engaged with God. They did not give up on faith, but threw themselves on the mercy of God. They flocked to churches. They read the Psalms.

The churches in and around Manhattan pitched in after 9/11, and, just as important, churches were the place of comfort across a whole nation when people came to worship with their hearts torn open. I will never forget our worship service immediately following that national tragedy. People in our church normally gather with energy and friendliness and glad chattiness. Not so on the weekend after 9/11. People arrived in quiet and stunned silence, a sobriety produced by trauma. Sorrow and fear and anger all swirling about and crashing into each other. On the afternoon of 9/11, which was a Tuesday, we had started to retool the worship service. We knew the music needed to be serious and soul searching. We sensed that the Psalms were the place to turn. That is where the hearts of people engage with the heart of God. The Psalms gave voice to the sorrow and rage in our hearts. I found a word in Psalm 25 that seemed to me to connect with the trauma we had just experienced: *treachery.*

> To you, O LORD, I lift up my soul;
> in you I trust, O my God.
> Do not let me be put to shame,
> nor let my enemies triumph over me.
> No one whose hope is in you
> will ever be put to shame,
> but they will be put to shame
> who are treacherous without excuse.

In a time of crisis, church leaders are responsible not just to provide comfort but to offer interpretation. People want to know "Will we be okay?" But they also want to know "What does all this mean?" Pastors and other church leaders are there to address both questions. We should never offer up easy answers or clichés. But we should assume that people are wondering in their hearts, *What is this all about?* On 9/11, there were no easy answers. On the weekend after 9/11, we all had to come to grips with one biblical truth: treachery is real.

COMMITTING TO A NEW INITIATIVE

One of the most exciting things to do in a church is to commit to a new initiative. When, through a variety of indicators, the church's leadership has the confidence to set off on a brand-new initiative, it is an exciting turning point. Such an initiative doesn't have to be a major paradigm-changing one, but rather something that affirms in the congregation that their church is alive and responsive and always looking to move out in new ways.

Last year I went to the twenty-fifth anniversary commemoration of a church of Laotian refugees in Milwaukee during which more than a thousand people celebrated with glee the great things God had done in their lives. This church is affiliated now with the Christian and Missionary Alliance, but it began with a couple of home fellowship groups in our church. Back in the early 1980s, when Laotian and Hmong refugees were looking for U.S. sponsors, two families in our church decided to make the commitment, but they included in this the involvement of the home fellowship they were connected to. My wife and I were in one of those groups, having joined the staff of our church when we were twenty-three and twenty-five years old. It was great. Occasionally taking care of the kids in this Laotian family, who had no familiarity with Western culture, including how to navigate our strange bathrooms, was an extraordinary cross-cultural experience.

John and his wife, Shirley, were the sponsors. At the time, John was the building manager of our church. John and Shirley are true authentic servants. They are simply willing to do whatever God wants them to do. And so, when the number of sponsored refugee families began to swell, and a pressing need for a real community among them developed, John and Shirley were catalysts in the birth of a new church, which quickly became two: a Laotian congregation and a Hmong. What began as a grassroots movement continued to develop, and more families were sponsored, as a church building in Milwaukee was purchased and as these new congregations grew and matured. Today John and Shirley live in east Asia, where they have been serving for the past two decades.

Committing to a new initiative is a powerful cohesive force, and sometimes more so when the ideas for the initiative come from the bottom up rather than from the top down.

IN PRACTICE—COHESIVE IDEAS FOR A WHOLE CHURCH

1. Determine the values that underlie the ministry of your church.
2. Keep communication flowing! When you think you've communicated enough, you have probably not yet done even half as much as should be done.
3. Use every means possible to communicate: verbal, print, Web site, e-mail. Repeat the main messages many times.
4. Treat people with respect when you communicate with them. Use straight talk. Never say what is untrue, but observe proper boundaries of confidentiality, which everyone would expect for themselves.
5. Put time into a quality annual congregational meeting, vision-casting event, or celebration.
6. Put pivotal communications in print. Go "on the record" when there is a key issue in the air, when every word you may say will count.
7. Determine which ministries of your church are the hub of the wheel—the common experience of the shared life (worship and sermon, for instance)—and invest time and effort to embrace the Whole Church in those experiences.
8. Tell stories of God's work in your church! Stories of grace, forgiveness, endurance, faith, and integrity remind people that this is why the church exists. Cohesion happens when we are drawn together by a high vision.

9. Keep the mission of the church central. Purpose draws people together. Your church may have a mission statement, or maybe your focus is on the mission as defined by Jesus: "make disciples."

10. Use mission as a way to filter out diversions and distractions. Use mission as a way to call people to peace when they are squabbling over things that don't matter.

11. Deal maturely and calmly with criticism. Let people who are bent out of shape have an opportunity to speak their piece to the appropriate leader(s). But then let them know that their views will be folded in with lots of other input. Critics have a right to be heard; they do not have a right to expect change based on their opinions alone.

12. Treat change as an opportunity for cohesion by making the case for how it will improve the ministry.

13. Take ample time for large changes. Build consensus from the center out. A major capital campaign or change of church government may take a year or more to prepare properly.

14. Tragedy often brings people together. A compassionate, broad-based response in a church will remind people why the church exists.

15. Organize almost all ministries as team efforts; develop teamwork as a core value; seek ways for teams to evaluate their strengths and weaknesses.

16. Give leaders the inside track on new thinking and upcoming developments (for instance, do a twice-monthly e-mail to all leaders and call it "The Inside Track").

17. Involve an ample base of leadership in upcoming changes. Ownership is key.

18. Give opportunities for leaders to share with other leaders their joys and struggles in their ministries.

19. Pull church staff together weekly for a substantial staff meeting (two to three hours). Make it half discussion and study, half business.

20. Find two excellent books on church ministry to have leaders read together in the next six to twelve months.

21. Hold a twenty-minute all-staff meeting that truly includes every staff member at every level. Use the time for a briefing on

what happened the previous week and what is coming up. Have someone tell an encouraging story. Stick to the twenty minutes.

22. Develop a church board that sees itself as the sounding board for important policy matters, but even more as the foundational support for the church staff.

23. Let leaders know when they do something right, not just when they do something wrong.

24. Review the church's values, mission, and strategies several times a year.

25. Regularly reinforce with leaders the core values of your church. Congratulate and encourage when those values have been displayed with integrity.

9

THE DYNAMICS OF
MOMENTUM

THE BIG IDEA
When a church allows itself to be propelled forward with
a momentum that God supplies, it is easier for the church
to hold together. An alive church is a church in motion. To
hold a church in suspension is a sure way for fractures to
take over.

A church is not a building, but people, right? Elemental stuff.
Sunday School 101. That is not the whole story, however. A church
is a body of people *in motion;* if there is no motion, it is not really
a church, but the breathless corpse of what used to be a church.
Whole Churches look for ways in which to keep the parts of the
body in motion. They don't let its muscles atrophy. They know
that a living community does not stand in one place.

Churches in motion have a clear sense of work to be done.
They work up a sweat as they wield their spiritual gifts as tools,
as opposed to treating spiritual gifts as decorations. Churches
in motion are steady, not frenetic. They know that overactivity
doesn't get the work done better or faster, but is more like the
nervous energy of a person who has a problem with hyperactivity.

When I was in high school, one of my best friends taught me
how to downhill ski. Now because he wasn't a professional instructor and because he had been known to play practical jokes on me,
I took with some skepticism the instructions he gave me at the top of
the hill as I looked down what seemed to be a certain path to death.

"Stay over your skis and lean into it," he said. "Your instinct will be to lean back on the skis, but you will have no control that way."

I found out—the hard way—that he was right. I leaned back, just as he had told me not to, and as a result I had no control, rapidly accelerating. After I removed myself from the entanglement of the shrubbery in which I had become caught at the bottom of the hill, I was ready either to pack it up or to try my friend's technique. Sure enough, when I wasn't afraid and leaned forward, I picked up momentum nicely but controllably. And with just the right amount of momentum, I was able to cut the skis into the snow, turning at will. Next stop: the Olympics.

Churches need momentum. Not so much that they careen out of control down the hill, but enough so that there is motion and forward progress.

So what does a church in motion look like? And how do the dynamics of momentum help a church be a Whole Church?

MOMENTUM AS ENTHUSIASM

It is hard not to be enthusiastic about enthusiasm—that is, unless it is disingenuous, contrived, or an end onto itself. Real enthusiasm within a church is that experience in which people are eagerly interested in something, enjoying the rightness and goodness of it, sensing forward motion because of it.

The root meaning of *enthusiasm* is "to be possessed by a god" (Greek *enthous*, from the words *theos*, "god," and *en* "in"). The word may be rooted in Greek mythology, but we can latch onto the idea of a church today being so filled by God that there is an eager enjoyment—a true enthusiasm—that people experience when a church is moving forward. But we must remember this: enthusiasm as a feeling is not what moves a church forward; the feeling is the by-product of a true experience of being carried along by God. If we believe that we as church leaders are merely purveyors of good feelings, then we might as well join the motivational speakers' circuit. There are techniques to get people whipped up with the mere feeling of enthusiasm, but the call that we have as leaders is to get people divinely motivated, to be "en-thused," filled with God. (This is a proper biblical concept, easily traced when you study "the fullness of Christ" and other similar expressions, a fruitful study for any church leader.[1])

Enthusiasm is the aftereffect when we establish forward motion and when we celebrate the motion in the past that brought us to the place we are today.

Years ago we decided that our church's annual congregational meeting needed to be transformed. For years it had served the purpose of the obligatory business meeting of the church. The faithful core members of the church attended, dutifully following along with the budget presentation, asking questions along the way. The annual congregational meeting held the potential of being spicy, too. If someone wanted to get feisty about the cost of replacing carpeting or, better yet, why someone was let go from the staff, the ACM was a chance at the big microphone.

The congregation left the annual meeting somewhat gratified, but rarely inspired. Enthusiasm was just not the typical by-product of this important gathering. The transformation of the annual congregational meeting came when it was decided that this once-a-year gathering of the membership of the church should be a celebration and a vision-casting experience. From there it was not hard to piece together a two-hour program that included robust storytelling of the accomplishments and poignant moments of the past year and testimonies of God's greatness. The forward-looking part of the evening became a time to focus on two or three main elements of vision for the upcoming year. The whole evening was wrapped in praise and prayer, preceded by a come-one, come-all supper and dessert on a special theme. This description doesn't do it justice, but suffice it to say that any church can put together an annual celebration event that informs and inspires the committed core of the church. In a day when we are all enthusiastic about the opportunities to connect with outsiders, it is important to preserve some of the quality experiences due the insiders.

Enthusiasm does not depend on a large congregational event, of course. Most of the excitement and satisfaction of good ministry in a church happens out in the extended ministry. People have many opportunities to celebrate: when a team volunteering to play softball at a local prison returns home, when a small group welcomes a missionary for whom it has been praying, when a children's camp ends with a special offering to support a local clinic, when a group of high school seniors has their last meeting as a group. And, of course, if worship is about participating in the fullness of Christ, then every weekend there is an opportunity to become en-thused and to know that in the enthusiasm, God is supplying more spiritual energy in the momentum of our lives.

MOMENTUM AS GROWTH

Churches must hold two truths in tension: stability and motion. We believe in stability because churches are based on changeless truths and an immutable (changeless) God, so they can offer the kind of stability that other organizations in our lives cannot offer. In the ancient church, it was taken as a maxim that there is nothing new under the sun. Innovation was not a positive concept, but instead the label for an idea that must be rejected because if it were valid, it would have held true generations earlier. Because we are so enamored with innovation today, it is easy for us to ridicule this conservative mind-set without considering its value—that there are some things that do not change and should not change. If you've ever thought that maybe we are expecting too much change, darting from one fad to the next or idolizing innovation, you may be sensing in yourself that proper conserving instinct that keeps us safe from ourselves. If you find yourself always looking at books published only in the last six months and wondering where the really good books are, you may be pleasantly surprised when you read something written fifty years ago by C. S. Lewis or three hundred years ago by a Puritan and find rock-solid ground beneath your feet. The word *conservative* may carry a lot of baggage, but almost no one can argue against the positive value of our instinct to conserve what is good.

But if we focus only on stability and conserving the past, we miss the steady, progressive momentum all churches must have. We miss the dynamic of growth. As a living organism, a church must grow (develop, adapt, evolve, mature, progress, expand). Our understanding of growth in our churches should parallel how growth works in the created order. In the first twenty years of my life, I grew physically, intellectually, and morally. Then I got married, eventually had kids—I was growing socially. Now at fifty-plus I am trying to prevent myself from growing around the middle, but I'm at a whole new stage of growth spiritually and intellectually. Taking what I've learned over the years, what I've experienced in the church, and the network of people I've developed,

I'm seeing things I've never seen before, learning things I couldn't have learned before.

So it is with our churches. In some phases of life, the focus is particularly on numeric growth. At other times it is on leadership growth or spiritual renewal or growth through crisis. The best scenario, of course, is that we are growing in all these ways at all times. Sometimes growth can be dramatic (as when there is a spike in attendance when a new facility is opened up), but oftentimes it is incremental, even imperceptible. As I write this I'm looking out a window at a maple tree that is growing as I watch it. Hour by hour as I sit here, it's not looking very different, because this growth is incremental. But make no mistake, the roots of this tree are strong, the fibers of the trunk are strong and flexible, the crown is thick and rich with life. Its growth is good *because* it is steady and incremental. It's very different from the birch tree a few feet over, which I planted a few years ago. Birches, like all trees of the poplar family, grow fast. They jump up and fill out. But this birch will probably blow over in a windstorm in a couple of decades, whereas the maple will likely last generations. Do we want to build churches that are maples or birches?

Growth is good, if it is good growth. Cancer is growth—the uncontrolled division of abnormal cells in the body—but the kind of growth that will kill you. Good growth in a church will always develop along the patterns of good relationships, good theology, and good structure.

And good growth will always be multidimensional—in people, in depth, in the forms of ministry, in the teaching of the church. Just as a human body grows in all its systems, there is no one growth experience that will put a church in motion or cause it to mature. There are dozens of ways for any church to foster an extended season of growth.

Here are some practical examples of good growth as a church in motion:

A church grows by developing new connecting points that did not exist before with a certain group—for instance, an outreach to twenty-something men and women via a new midweek worship-teaching-fellowship evening.

A church grows by beginning a ministry to senior citizens that focuses on substantive spiritual growth, not just social gatherings.[2]

A church grows by finding partnerships with overseas ministries and developing long-term relationships with them.

A church grows by extending itself in a multisite strategy—not one copied from another church, but rather one that is suited to the culture of that church.

A church grows by offering a twelve-week Sunday night lecture series exploring Christianity and culture.

A church grows by diversifying its staff.

MOMENTUM AS MOVING OUT

A church can be and must be a living, breathing, moving body, and one of the ways in which it can do that is to be "moving out." That means seeing a wider horizon for ministry, launching into territory previously unexplored, serving Christ, and serving the community in bold and imaginative new ways. Moving out happens when a church's leaders believe that the home ministry is a secure and stable base from which to extend into the community and the culture with effective witness. Churches don't move out when they think that so much repair and refinement needs to be done at home that they are not ready to extend. But, of course, with such a mind-set that day of readiness never comes. Churches are not preparing for a landing invasion into the world; they already are in the world, the battle with evil and sin has already been joined, and new missions need to be released every day.

Some churches that actually change locations out of a sense of mission are literally moving out. In years past in metropolitan areas, such movement has often taken the form of churches' buying a patch of land out in the suburbs or on the edge of the countryside and relocating. But everybody recognizes this as a mixed bag. Churches can gain a great new foothold, and sometimes comfortable acreage allowing for physical growth, but everyone worries about whether these churches are abandoning the core of their communities to build on the comfortable edges. So some bold churches today are taking the interior territory, moving into the city rather than away from it. Other churches are establishing satellite ministries in the city. But one of the best ways for a church to break out of its own neighborhood, to move out across its communities, is to inspire and empower a movement of community engagement.

Moving out is a much wider dynamic than the physical relocation of churches. Moving out is about spiritual momentum. A church moves out when it adopts effective and strategic overseas projects or missions. This may begin with writing a check, but it is a shame if it stops there. When a church carefully chooses its mission connections and develops deep and sustained relationships with them, then it is moving out. Making financial donations is a significant way for a church to extend itself, but when there is a personal dimension and a personal connection, that takes reaching out to a whole new level.

MOMENTUM AS WORK

I love the story Garrison Keillor tells of an old Norwegian bachelor farmer visiting the big city, Minneapolis, and being exposed to the peculiar ways of city folks—especially young urban professionals. He is riding in the car around the lakes of the city, seeing dozens of people running on paths around the lakes. His only comment: "What are those people doing? Can't they get work?"

It never would have occurred to my grandfather to use a treadmill or purchase an exercise video. You sweat when you work. For him that meant hauling large boxes of stock for the small grocery store he owned, butchering the meat for the cold case, mowing the grass, rebuilding broken shelves, sweeping and mopping the floor at closing time well after dark. He was strong and alive. His work was his dignity and all the exercise he ever needed.

As church leaders interested in the strength, health, and virility of our churches, we need to make sure we are not looking for the technique that produces health, but rather the purpose for the church's existence, the mission it is called to, and understand that *a church at work* is a church getting stronger and stronger.

When I talk to church leaders, there is no biblical passage I use more often than Ephesians 4:11–13:

> It was he who gave some to be apostles, some to be prophets, some to be evangelists, and some to be pastors and teachers, to prepare God's people for works of service, so that the body of Christ may be built up until we all reach unity in the faith and in the knowledge of the Son of God and become mature, attaining to the whole measure of the fullness of Christ. . . . [S]peaking the truth in love, we will in all things grow up into him who is the Head, that is, Christ. From him the whole body, joined and held together by every supporting ligament, grows and builds itself up in love, as each part does its work.

What a great passage! God gave leaders to the church so that they could prepare God's people to work. But not the kind of work that produces the poison of self-righteousness (from which any believer and any church is always only one short stop away). Any church leader can work in such a way that he or she gets a lot of attention and admiration—but in a way that is as vacuous (and dangerous) as the work of the Pharisees. Ephesians 4 defines and bounds our work so that it is purposeful and life giving—though it will mean blood and sweat and tears unlike any other work we will ever do. This just may be the most important biblical passage church leaders need to daily shape their activities and priorities. The essential principles of the passage break down like this:

1.   God "gives" leaders to the church ("he gave some to be apostles, some to be . . ."). But be careful before striking a pose as if you are God's gift to humanity. The church doesn't need prima donnas; it needs foremen for the work crews. What a privilege to believe that you have been given by God to the church for his highest purposes in the world!

2.   Leaders are to "prepare God's people." The Greek word translated here as "prepare" is used in Matthew 4:21 for the fishermen "mending" their nets. It is also used in Hebrews as God "fashioning" the universe in creation (Heb. 11:3). So when we "prepare" God's people, it means we have the great privilege of

helping fashion their lives into Christlikeness, and repairing the broken parts of their lives. It is people-investment pure and simple. But it is preparation for a purpose.

3.   "Works of service"—that is what we are preparing people for. The church is not a country club; it is a boot camp preparing people for battle. The church is not a stage show; it is a university preparing people for life with a full and detailed understanding of truth so that they can be agents of truth. The church is a hospital, a place of healing so that the healed can become healers themselves. The church is a guild, continually preparing the next generation of apprentices for the work that lies ahead.

4.   "Works of service" means that service defines work. Doing work for work's sake does not accomplish anything enduring unless it is service, which is work done *for someone.* A church picks up real momentum when ever-increasing numbers of people start to serve. Service breaks us out of lethargy. Service gets our minds off our own comfort. Service orients us to the dynamic changes of life (because we cannot predict when the next funeral is going to come, or the next family in need, or the next unforeseen opportunity to speak into our communities). Service exercises the muscles of a church. It makes a church breathe deeply the breath of the Spirit. It builds an unassailable witness to the community.

5.   Works of service "build up" the body of Christ. There are those body builders who work out in gyms for countless hours, refining the shape of every muscle, sculpting the body in ways that seem unnatural, and always ready for the show. That is not what building the body of Christ looks like. Think of someone you know who works with his hands, lifts heavy objects in his work, puts in an honest day's work, and doesn't watch his calories because he uses all of them in his work. His body is strong; his coordination is excellent. This is what churches are to be. But it doesn't happen overnight. As leaders we have the privilege of gradually introducing more and more people to the pleasure and the cost of service. It doesn't matter whether it is service within the believing community or outside. In many ways the real growth happens when

the work is outside. But gradually you see strength. At first there may be fatigue and pain. The muscle of a church builds gradually. But once the muscle is there, it has a way of looking for the next opportunity to stretch.

6.   And then comes this bonus: "unity in the faith and in the knowledge of the Son of God." Faith that works (as in the epistle of James) has a self-authenticating quality that pulls people together. It is "unity in the faith," not just in the sense of unity of belief, but unity in faith-experience. When, for instance, a community disaster occurs and believers spring into action, putting their faith to work, they look around at their fellow believers and realize that they have been mobilized for a significant work of the moment. They are together in the work, and drawn together in the faith. It is work that is ennobling for the workers, lifesaving for the victims of the disaster, and encouraging for the community watching. This unity in the faith is also unity "in the knowledge of the Son of God." There are many ways in which we know Christ, and one of the most transformative ways is to know Christ in the work we do together, which reminds us that Jesus has called us to a great mission. We, like Jesus' first disciples, know him as we walk on the trail, enter the communities, watch God's power unleashed, talk to him about it afterwards. The work of the church is a momentum that carries us into the next village, even when we don't know what awaits us there.

7.   We become "mature." The word *teleios* means "complete" or "whole." Complete in the sense that it has available to it *all the resources Christ intends the church to have or to need.* We have the gospel of grace, the means and the motive to forgive, a mandate for love. We have the power to stand up to evil, and the tools to resist temptation. We have hope that gives strength in the face of disease and death. We have truth, not for pride and exclusion, but for discernment and wisdom that is generous and outward looking. We have a God-defined value system that does not diminish human nature, but elevates it. We have a life that raises us above prejudices and small-mindedness. This is what it means to become mature or "complete." And it is what it means to become whole. A Whole Church is one which realizes that it has been given everything it needs in Christ, even though it continues on a path of

acquiring the fullness of Christ, and will always be working against the forces of fragmentation arising directly out of human nature.

8. "Attaining to the whole measure of the fullness of Christ" is the ultimate goal. "The fullness of Christ" points us to the life and character of Jesus, who came "from the Father, full of grace and truth." That is one way of stating the goal for the Whole Church: to be full of grace and truth. Grace that gives and truth that protects. Or we could look at the fruit of the Spirit (Gal. 5) and ask, Is there a better description of the character of Jesus, and the character of a Whole Church? "Love, joy, peace, patience, kindness, goodness, faithfulness, gentleness, self-control."

9. "From him the whole body, joined and held together by every supporting ligament, grows and builds itself up in love." The Whole Church is possible because of Christ, from whom the whole body grows in love. Take a look around. What possible hope do you have to be "joined and held together" with your fellow leaders and your fellow members in the body without some strong God-designed ligaments that support the whole body? Oftentimes leaders are those ligaments.

10. The passage begins with "works of service" and ends with the body that "grows and builds itself up in love, as each part does its work."

This is the church at work. This is the church in motion.

It is best not to look for any one thing to propel a church forward. Momentum builds. And the energy of the movement should not be solely that of a visionary leader; it should be a movement of the Holy Spirit that becomes the vision of many people.

IN PRACTICE—COHESIVE IDEAS FOR A WHOLE CHURCH

1. Develop a culture of servanthood! When people really believe that "the members are the ministers" and a movement of service develops, the sky is the limit.

2. Keep teaching about servanthood. Celebrate it. Reward it. Frame service as the true evidence that God is at work.

3. Make prayer a high priority at a time of new initiatives. People need to know that forward-looking ideas are shaped by a devotion to God's ways of working.

4. Once every five to ten years, initiate a process among leaders to recast the vision of the church. Come up with a list of eight to twelve significant initiatives that will spread out over the following five to ten years.

5. Once a year, initiate a process among leaders to determine the major emphases for the following year. Focus on one to three main emphases.

6. Have an all-church celebration and vision-casting meeting one evening each year. This may be a new event or a transformed annual congregational meeting if that is the practice of your church.

7. Treat any large-scale project that the church takes on (building construction or renovation, reorganizing of ministries, change of staff, and so on) as an opportunity to get people en-thused.

8. To generate enthusiasm about financial giving, celebrate with the congregation the ministry that is being accomplished through giving. Tell concrete stories of accomplishments: a successful children's camp, a new church plant, building improvements, community outreach. Understand what is important to the congregation, and emphasize those things.

9. Do not wait until you are behind budget to communicate about giving. The message about finances should be more positive than negative.

10. Look for leaders with pioneer spirits.

11. Look for leaders with the gift of creativity, and give them latitude to create. Better to make a creative mistake once in a while than to linger in mediocrity.

12. Give to leaders the freedom to try new ideas. Not everything needs to be controlled from the top. There is nothing wrong with an effort to try something new that doesn't work out, as long as the potential damage is not great.

13. Don't play it too safe with new ideas. Be willing to take risks.

14. Set budget goals that challenge a congregation to grow, but not numbers that are purely arbitrary.
15. Understand the history and patterns of your congregation with regard to what motivates them to invest in the ministry.
16. Arrange testimonials in the worship service about accomplishments that glorify God.
17. Study the ministry of other churches to learn about how they gain momentum.
18. When you look at other model churches, discover the principles behind what they accomplish, not just the actions they took.
19. Inculcate a pioneer spirit in the children and youth of the church. Help them see the church as an ever-growing and developing community.
20. Have the courage to discontinue programs that have long ceased to be effective. This is hard for churches to do, even though churches should know that corpses deserve a proper burial.
21. If you do discontinue a program, do not disenfranchise the remnant of leaders who are still invested in it. Communicate with them why discontinuance is necessary. If they are disappointed, acknowledge their feelings and express gratitude for their service.
22. Help displaced leaders find their next venue of ministry.
23. Anticipate the next phase of momentum for your church. Start talking about next phases of ministry, not when energy in the church has been depleted, but when a phase has crested (five years? seven years? ten years?).
24. Develop a church board that understands steady momentum.
25. Use an outside speaker to rally the congregation for a new initiative.

10

CREATING A
CULTURE OF CHANGE

THE BIG IDEA
All churches change. When a church does not foster a culture of strategic change and incremental change, it is likely to go through disruptive change.

It was called Pilgrim Community Church, and it was situated on Main Street. How much more of an anchor can you have than that? But that was precisely the problem: almost half the people in the church knew that over a long period of years, the church had gone from being an anchor that holds and secures to an anchor that limits and constricts. The church was weighed down by its own heritage. So some of the people in the church wanted the anchor to be lifted and for the ship to set out on the high seas of new ministry opportunities in the new millennium. These reformers wanted to see the worship updated; they wanted to experiment with new forms of ministry and in many ways to get the ministries they had already developed in the city and in the marketplace to be endorsed by the church leaders. They wanted the real issues of life in the twenty-first century to be addressed, and not just a continual solidifying of the past. The younger associate pastors on the church's staff resonated with that desire, but the senior pastor was wary of what looked like a move to compromise the principles of the church.

This church could have been called Redeemer Lutheran or Bethel United Methodist or First Baptist Church—the dynamics are the same no matter what the denominational identity of the church.

We all struggle with change.

But let's step back. Here are four universal dynamics:

1. We all struggle with change.
2. We all will change—whether we choose to or not.
3. It is better for a church to create a culture of intentional change, rather than passively succumb to imposed change.
4. If we do have a culture of change, then we are much less likely to struggle with change.

Pilgrim Community Church did change. Not because its leaders plotted a course of change, but because those longing for change left the church, family by family, and connected with other congregations. And when two-thirds of the people had gone, it dawned on the leaders that they should have adapted, but by then it was too late because they were left with a core of people committed to fossilizing the church. The church shrunk in the community until it was mostly spoken of in the past tense.

Change holds the potential to fragment a church or to be one of the most exciting cohesive experiences a church can go through. For change to be positive, we must embrace it.

CHANGE WILL UPSET PEOPLE

The first order of business is to clear up our confusion about change. Church leaders need to reinforce two principles continuously: change is a good thing (and a biblical principle), but change does not mean compromising principle. Change compromises the gospel only if the essential faith and message of the church are abandoned or twisted.

Change means adjusting, adapting, modifying, revising, refining, refashioning, revamping, reorganizing, reordering, transforming, evolving, growing. How can change not be a good thing? There are many church leaders who will look at change in that light and agree with its necessity, but they are stuck on one thing: "Some people won't like it if we change." Some people will complain. Some people may make a big stink about it. Some people will stop giving. Some people may even leave the church. So these leaders don't change, or they procrastinate to the point that the change never happens. In some cases, they dare not change the least little thing. And all the reasons why change was necessary in the first place get buried.

Here is a tough question for any leader: So what if people get upset about change? So what if they leave the church and go to a different, more "changeless, timeless" church? It's not that you want them to leave. And you certainly have many means of joining with these people, respectfully hearing their concerns, and hoping that they will stay with the church even when the changes take place. But when all is said and done, people who say that they will leave rather than tolerate change under any circumstances must be left to leave.

I find that there is a lot of confusion about the issue of people "leaving" the church. My heart is torn when I hear about people who have had such a difficult experience that one day they just don't show up, and they never come back. This is a true spiritual crisis— when people say that they are giving up not just on the church but on God. That is where the shepherd's drive to find the one in a hundred who has wandered off must kick in. And we often don't know—did the person give up on God because he or she gave up on a church that was disappointing to him or her? Or is it that the spiritual crisis was between the person and God, and giving up the church was the aftereffect? Very often what is revealed is that people who are bitterly upset with the church have some terrible difficulty going on in their lives that nobody knew about. These people are in life crises, and they project that on the church, wondering why nobody is reaching out to them at their time of need (and often others should have noticed that the crisis was personal). Or someone rails against the church and leaves in a huff, and only later is it revealed that he or she was having an affair or some other moral crisis.

It is very different when someone says that he or she is going to start to attend the church across town because it is a better spiritual environment for him or her. Over the years, I have had many discussions with people who say they are moving on. Sometimes it's because their families are at a stage where it is better to find a church closer to where they live. Sometimes it's because they have a perfect opportunity to use their gifts in service in a different congregation. Some people reach a point in their lives when they simply want to be part of a smaller congregation—and when they get there, they flourish. We encourage people to leave when we are planting a new church and need a core of pioneers who will be the base of the new congregation.

How much better it is for church leaders to give people their blessings when they decide to be part of a different congregation, for *good* and *reasonable* reasons. Here is where we have to decide, Do we or do we not believe that the body of Christ is one thing? Do we really believe that different Christian congregations are different parts of one body? Can anyone imagine the Apostle Paul getting upset if someone moved from one house church in Rome over to a different one for very good reasons? Do we believe in the Whole Church?

To get to that mind-set, we have to give up our conscious or subconscious hold on any sense of ownership of church members. We have to give up any sense that our success as one church or our worth as leaders is tied into the exact attendance numbers.

On the one hand, every church should want to grow out of an unwavering passion to reach out to those who are unmoored and detached, floating free in life without a spiritual home, without Christ. Jesus' command to "make disciples" couldn't be clearer. We want to grow, not just for the sake of the numbers, but for the sake of the numbers of people receiving the immense blessings of moving into the kingdom of Christ. The *Titanic* has sunk, the lifeboats are in the water, as many as can be saved should be saved.

On the other hand, there are many factors that influence church attendance at any given point in time. In our city, for decades there were very few evangelical churches with effective ministries. The last twenty years have seen dramatic changes. There are good, fresh, new churches popping up all over the place. The greater Milwaukee area was like a field ready to be harvested. As a consequence, many longtime members of our church have ventured out as pioneers into these new settings—a good thing. A great thing. The real way to measure the growth of the church as the body of Christ is to consider the growth of the cluster of congregations in a given area, not just measure the dimensions of one congregation.

CHANGING THE MESSAGING
WITHOUT CHANGING THE MESSAGE

There is great confusion in churches about changing the message of the church. There can be heartrending angst in some people if they believe that their church has compromised or given up on the gospel. It is only human to see some change on the surface and be worried about what is going on below the surface. How big is that iceberg under there, and will it tear a hole in the side of our ship? Some examples:

The pastor reads from a translation of the Bible not usually used (let's say, a more understandable colloquial translation), and some people believe God's Word has been compromised.

The church changes the appearance of the bulletin handed out each week. It's got a contemporary look, very snappy, very much in line with the best print communications in the culture, and some people see the change as bringing the ways of the world into the church.

A church's leader proposes changing the name of the church from MacArthur Avenue Baptist Church to New Life Community because most of the people coming to the church now don't come from a Baptist background, and the church moved from MacArthur Avenue to a new location ten years ago. The thought of changing the church's name is almost unthinkable to people who have been attending for ten years or more.

The speaker in the worship service decides to use video clips as illustrations, and letters come in the next week about how using a clip from "that" movie compromised the whole sermon.

For the first time, a professional ballet artist in the church choreographs a dance depicting the life of Ruth, to be performed while a song about Ruth is sung. It is stunningly moving to almost everybody, but some are angry that dance has been introduced into a worship service.

Now maybe you read those examples and thought that such changes would produce similar reactions in your church, or you may be thinking that you are so far down the road on changes that this is kindergarten stuff, that you can introduce almost anything and people won't flinch. But the main point is this: change is significant. Sometimes church leaders are frustrated that congregations won't tolerate change with level-headed grace. Sometimes congregations wish that their leaders would get on the stick and start making necessary changes. And there are some churches that change without anybody batting an eye, but someone should have because the church did stray from its core principles and biblical standards; it's just that nobody really noticed because in the culture of those churches, innovation always trumps everything else.

So what about changing the messaging without changing the message? We do live in a world that is in the midst of a communications revolution. The technology of Gutenberg's press back in the early 1400s changed the world because ideas could start to spread like wildfire, even though it was by reproducing one page of text after another under the press. (Martin Luther's ideas, for instance, were rapidly copied, and the pamphlets made their way via the waterways of Europe within weeks, having a profound impact on the thinking of the leaders of the day.)

Today I write an e-mail to those who subscribe to my list, hit Send, and it is "published" in the inboxes of thousands of people in dozens of countries all over the world. Churches of all sizes today have desktop publishing, resource-rich Web sites, and online teaching. People in many churches today assume that they can get the information they need in a couple of minutes because it will be posted on their church's Web site.

The messaging is changing, but that does not mean the message is. Even those who have insisted that in a postmodern era we have to tell Christian truth through the metanarrative of Scripture are not necessarily changing the message. To draw out the power of the narrative portions of Scripture, to depict the stories with vividness, is not to change the message but to rediscover it. Jesus, after all, is the preeminent storyteller of all time.

The message is changed, however, when people say that we must become skeptical of the very idea of truth. The message is changed when a new generation is so enamored with itself that it considers previous generations to be some earlier, more primitive stage of evolution. Interestingly, many younger church leaders today have taken a strong interest in the ancient church and the ancient ways. It's new to be old. And they have found that connecting with the ancient church through the creeds, the prayers, and some of the practices to be a rich and integrating experience. No wonder. It is the satisfaction that comes from participating in the Whole Church.

I have had many conversations with younger leaders, pointing out to them the pit into which many of us in the baby-boomer generation fell. We were the first generation to be given an identity. We were the subjects of sociological studies, cultural interpreters, and marketing expertise. We were taught to be self-conscious. And the downside of that was when we became self-absorbed, self-interested, and self-aggrandizing. The worst thing that ever happened to the baby-boom generation was to be told that we were "special." That made us feel privileged, and that is a curse we are still having to break in the church today. Imagine how awful it might be when we baby boomers are in our seventies and eighties. The potential for crankiness in the church will be at an all-time high.

But it doesn't have to be. I know many senior citizens who have decided that they stand for the Whole Church, not just because they want to be tolerant of people in their twenties, but because they love the dynamics of being in a multigenerational church. Their spirits rejoice in the hope that new generations are coming forward to carry on with the work and living the message. And it works the other way, too. There are younger people who don't always want to be just with people of their generation, but who take comfort from those who show stability in a very unstable culture.

STRATEGIC CHANGE

All churches will change. The issue is whether we will change intentionally, or resist change so that one day the change that inevitably does happen is disruptive, destructive change.

One approach to change is intentional, planned, prepared, and carefully executed. This is *strategic change*. Strategy is a plan of action designed to achieve a major or overall aim (in contrast with tactics, which are actions aimed at achieving a specific aim). Here are some examples of strategic changes for a church:

Once every five to ten years having a strategic planning process that defines the major initiatives of the church in the upcoming decade

Planning for a building expansion

Moving the location of the church

Working through a restructuring of the basic paradigm of leadership for a church

Changing a church's constitution

Attaching to or detaching from a denominational affiliation

Changing the fundamental paradigm of spiritual care in a congregation to small groups

Adopting a multisite strategy

Changing international outreach from a traditional missions model to a direct-relationship model

Investing in outposts of ministry in the local community

Changing the major focus of the church's ministry

Sometimes the line between strategy and tactics is blurred, but these labels don't matter that much in a church. The main issue is that when church leaders are contemplating a sweeping and major change, they need to know that the change is strategic and to prepare for the change properly so that it doesn't become an experience of division in the church. Major changes will always produce the most anxiety and tension in a congregation, but when they are done right, strategic changes can launch a church to a whole new level of ministry.

A small group of leaders (or one leader) can decide on a strategic change, put it in motion, and let the chips fall where they may. If people don't like the changes, they can just leave. But there are better ways to enact strategic change.

The alternative is that leaders can see strategic change as a movement of the whole body, of the Whole Church. Courageous leaders will be willing to do the work of holding a body together through the strategic change.

Here are some elements of making a smooth strategic change:

Ownership. One leader or a small group may be the core of change, but with a smart process and enough time, they can win over an ever-widening circle of people who see the wisdom of the idea and take ownership of it (which means investing in it, not just "buying in," and certainly more than acquiescing).

Communication. Change requires careful, accurate, thorough, honest, and frequent communication: verbal communication to the whole congregation, word-of-mouth communication generated by giving subgroups in the church and leaders the essential points and stories, media communications (Web site, video, photography, text-messaging, e-mail), and written communication. It is hard to overestimate the importance of written communication. We should not let anybody tell us that because we live in an age of the image, the word does not matter to people. Most hard information people get is in written form. If, for instance, you explain a major change in the church in a printed piece that has three thousand carefully crafted words describing the purpose, intent, outlines, timetable, and funding of an initiative, that piece can be read and reread. It can be passed on to others. It will be referred to months down the road when people get fuzzy in their thinking about what the deal was in the first place. You are "on record" when you commit to print. When changes occur that produce problems, one of the most frequent complaints is, "But you never told us" or "We didn't understand" or "What we were told was . . ." This is the reason to communicate, communicate, communicate. It takes work, but the dividends are great.

Reasonable implementation. Leaders who are eager for change and who push for the change based on their drive and impulses very often produce unnecessary cracks and fissures in the church. Simple arrogance says, *I want change, and I want it now.* Wisdom says, *We need to change, and we are willing to be as diligent and as patient as it takes to do it right.* Leaders need to consult with the major people who will be affected by the change. They need to understand the work it will take for them to implement the change. Unlike a business or a military unit, a church has values rooted in human respect. A change is good if it moves people as people, not as chess pieces on a board. So church leaders need to work with multiple layers of influencers to make sure that a major change is done right. Strategy is meaningless if it is not matched with appropriate tactics.

Carefully planned timing. Some leaders, by nature and temperament, tend to be impatient or quick to the draw, and want strategic change to happen as soon as possible. Many other leaders have a cautious temperament and err on the side of being not decisive enough, or of wanting to ensure that everybody is happy before a change is made. Neither extreme makes for good strategic change. Every change has a different ideal timing profile.

CONTINUAL INCREMENTAL CHANGE

Strategic change is not the only path toward growth and development in the life of a church. Perhaps even more important than strategic turning points are the process and culture of *continual incremental change.* This is change that happens not once every five or ten years, but month after month, along a rising grade of perpetual improvement and adaptation.

The very idea of incremental change, of change happening gradually and progressively over an extended period of time, will strike some leaders as halfhearted or overly cautious. But here is where leaders need to their hold their egos and ambitions in abeyance and think hard about the minds and spirits of the congregations they lead. Church communities want to grow; they do not want to be yanked around. Their instincts on this matter often protect us as leaders from our own independent ambitions and impulsive ideas.

If a church develops a culture of *continual incremental change,* then it is less likely that sudden, radical change will be needed with the passage of time. Continual incremental change means that every area of the church is always changing, bit by bit. Over time, significant change happens, and it is possible for the congregation to understand the sensibleness of it because they see the change as occurring in steps. What a shame if, out of mere impatience, we don't use continual incremental change as a major way for our churches to grow and change.

Continual incremental change is growth. Like a human being, like a family, a church is designed by God to be a growing entity.

God saw fit to have human beings grow from infancy through childhood through adolescence through early adulthood, adulthood, and elder adulthood. For some reason, God chose incremental change as the model of how he works. Growth is a miracle. It is the way we learn about the spark of life, early dependence, independence and responsibility, dependence again. Growth is how we learn about injury and disease and healing. Growth is the way we progress educationally from elemental lessons to refined understanding to deep knowledge. So it is in the church.

Continual incremental change is less disruptive and jarring to a congregation. Let's take worship as an example. For the past couple of decades, many churches have agonized over the so-called worship wars. Does a church stay with the forms of worship it has employed for decades, or move into newer forms of worship? Some churches have decided not to change anything. Others have decided to offer different times and places for a "contemporary service." Others have started new churches in order to offer the newer forms. And some churches have decided on a course of continual incremental change. That was the path Elmbrook Church chose many years ago. The church's leaders decided that having a multigenerational congregation was not impossible, and chose a Whole Church model of worship. What made this possible was continual incremental change. Every year, we introduced some new and creative element of worship: drama, creative storytelling of global outreach via video, interpretive dance, creative elements in the sermons; we lessened the amount of performed music, increased the congregational praise. With every passing year the worship has changed—incrementally, and according to new gifts, opportunities, and creative ideas.

Continual incremental change makes it more likely that the Whole Church can hang together. Change is inevitable. Change is necessary. The purposes and core practices of worship do not change, but there are always new forms to explore. The Great Commission does not change, but the way in which a church can proclaim the gospel to its community and engage in global mission is a continually evolving reality.

CHANGE AND THE GENERATIONS

In much of the discussion of church ministry today, it seems as though the idea of a multigenerational church has been forgotten. Or we have given up on the possibility. Culture is so bold and dynamic and imposing—how can it be possible for a church to have significant constituencies of young adults, middle-aged adults, and older adults? Can one church include people who think in postmodern, modern, and antimodern mind-sets?

Wise change management makes it possible for a Whole Church to remain multigenerational, which is an ideal that should not be discarded too quickly.

First of all, we should not assume that the changing culture is generation specific. Postmodernism is not simply the culture in which young adults move; it is the culture in which all of us live. Any person from any generation can come into the church a New Ager, an ultraconservative, a self-indulgent consumer, a political right-winger or left-winger, an Earth worshipper, or a Wall Street worshipper. If the biblical view of human nature and the soul is our beginning point, we will know that human beings have essentially the same needs, aspirations, fears, and potential vices and virtues. We will not assume that the only way for a church to coalesce is for it to be generation specific. The Whole Church is still possible.

Second, we should not assume that different generations are disinterested in each other. It certainly is true that when we act on our basic instincts, we choose to associate with people who are most like us. It is easier, more comfortable, less costly. But in the Whole Church we don't acquiesce to our basic instincts. It is fine to belong to peer groups. It is inevitable. But I know scores of young adults who really value the connection they have with the older generations. And I know that the seniors want to know what is going on in the lives of teens and young adults. They want to hear that there is hope for the next generation, and they are willing to hear heartbreaking news of the challenges younger people have, too. These are the impulses that reveal our desire to believe in the Whole Church, because peer groups are a dime a dozen in secular culture. The church offers something that transcends race, gender, social class, and generational differences.

I am so enthusiastic when I see a senior citizen working in our children's ministry, rocking an infant to sleep. Or when I learn that a group of twenty-somethings have had a years-long commitment to one night a week of service in a retirement home. I love the challenge of preaching to a congregation that includes children, teens, young adults, middle-aged adults, and older adults. I enjoy talking to young adults about what really matters to them in the church, and using what I learn from real people to modify what I read in many books by "experts." I learn so much when a teaching connects across the ages because the topic hits at something at the core of human nature—fear, pride, lack of confidence, guilt, and dozens of other issues. I am glad to have in this community called church the opportunity to have friends so different from myself.

At the bottom line is this question: Will we be bold enough to let God change our churches so that they are bigger and broader and wider than we could ever have imagined? Are we enthusiastic—really *en-thused*—about discovering what the Whole Church means today? And are we willing to really commit to building churches not on the basis of affinity but on the basis of reconciliation of people as different from each other as night and day?

- -
IN PRACTICE—COHESIVE IDEAS
FOR A WHOLE CHURCH
- -

1. Always use the word "change" as a positive term.
2. Talk about change frequently, so that it is not seen as a threat.
3. Teach the biblical concept of change (growth, new life, radical commitment, leading of the Spirit).
4. Celebrate change whenever it accomplishes something good in the church.
5. See worship as a central cohesive experience of the church, and as an opportunity for the church to experience continual incremental change.
6. Try new ways of reading Scripture in worship.
7. Try new forms of prayer in worship (extemporaneous if your tradition is set prayers; set prayers if your tradition has always been extemporaneous).

8. Try new ways of preaching: from notes, extemporaneous, from an outline.

9. Hire young. The composition of a church staff will increasingly drift older unless the church adds people on the younger side when new positions open. This is important not just for ministry staff but also for secretaries, custodians, or any area.

10. Have children's ministry and youth ministry leaders look at each new year as an opportunity to bring some incremental change.

11. Prepare for strategic change well ahead of time. Develop ownership of ideas from central leaders on out. Invite them into shaping the ideas.

12. Some major changes (for example, major building expansion, changing church government) take longer to develop. Initiate a significant new change by "dropping a pebble in the pool" and giving other leaders an opportunity to kick the idea around.

13. When decisive change is necessary, get the central leaders of the church on the same page, gain a solid commitment to rationale, and communicate respectfully to the congregation the need for the change.

14. Begin a process of incremental change in worship right now. Introduce new elements or new ways of using typical elements, one step at a time. Don't be rattled if a few people complain. Evaluate the changes based on spiritual benefit.

15. Study how other churches similar to your own have gone through changes.

16. Take ample time in making significant changes. Don't let a group of discontents rush an important process.

17. Don't communicate change to the congregation if you don't know the what, why, when, who, and how. It is not an advantage to a congregation if you say you know changes are necessary, but you have no idea what the changes will be.

18. Institute continual incremental change in a ministry area even before it is necessary. Making small steps of change normative is the best way to avoid having change viewed as a disruption.

19. Communicate, communicate, communicate—long before changes, during planning for change, during change. And don't forget to communicate after the change!

20. Use words other than "change": adapt, adjust, amend, modify, revise, remodel, refine reorder, reshape, refashion, redesign, restyle, revamp, rework, reorganize, vary, transform, transfigure, transmute, evolve.
21. Thank people who make sacrifices for the sake of necessary change. Be understanding about any sense of loss they may experience.
22. Help people understand change that may seem undesirable, but that is out of your control: a slumping economy, a changing neighborhood, a failed leader.
23. Work with second- and third-tier leaders as the key agents of change.
24. Dream about the possibilities of your church's ministry a decade down the road. Don't make commitments too far ahead of time, but let distant horizons be a positive motivation.
25. Make sure the ministry staff and governing board are always fully informed about upcoming changes.

CHURCH CRISES
THE MAKE-OR-BREAK MOMENTS

THE BIG IDEA
Crisis can make or break a community. If we assume crisis will happen in our churches, respond to it with faith and truth, and access all of God's gifts to get through the crisis, our churches will come out stronger.

We all—leaders and nonleaders alike—have personal experiences that shake us to the core. Experiences that will break us and threaten to shatter us, but that can strengthen us if we survive and grow. So it is with church congregations. Beyond personal crises, which happen every week in the lives of at least some people in a congregation, there are those crises that extend to the Whole Church. Sooner or later a church will feel the foundations shaken, and that is when we learn what we are made of, and whether we can engage with each other and with God at a time of need, or whether we end up a pile of rubble. Similar to an earthquake that makes some buildings sway and others break, community crises show us where our *koinonia* is strong and where it is weak.

CRISES OF THE WHOLE CHURCH

Here are some examples of crises in the Whole Church:

The moral failure of a pastor resulting in a sudden departure and trauma for the church

A case of embezzlement by a church office employee

An affair between two key leaders in the youth ministry

A pastor's suicide that no one saw coming

A separation and divorce between the senior pastor and his wife

A church fire that leaves the building uninhabitable for months

Gross vandalism of the church building that intentionally dese-crates the space and taunts the beliefs of the congregation

The forced removal of a pastor by denominational officials

A church split that finally occurs after years of division between two factions in the church

An ugly power struggle between the church board and staff

An untimely death in a beloved family from the church

I got off an airplane ready to settle in for an hour until the connecting flight. Turning on my cell phone, the text message function buzzed immediately, a message from my wife: SAD NEWS ABOUT MISSIONARIES. CALL. My stomach immediately felt twisted in a knot.

I called home. The initial news was sketchy. Two long-time church members, Warren and Donna, who were teaching agriculture in the north of Uganda, had been shot and killed by a band of men in a nighttime raid. Their house had been set afire, and when they emerged, they were gunned down.

Just a few weeks earlier, Warren and Donna had stood in front of our congregation being sent out with prayer. Everyone loved them. They were local farmers, and the kind of people anyone would love to have as a neighbor or relative. Every conversation I ever had with them left me feeling encouraged and brightened. They had served in the children's ministry for years, and surprised everybody when they told their friends that they had a growing desire to uproot and serve overseas as missionaries. The local paper ran an article about these small-town farmers going to Africa. It was a tough challenge. One day Warren held up a handful of dry Ugandan dust and let it pour through his fingers, telling a friend, "It's not like farming back in Wisconsin."

One of our pastors who knew Warren and Donna well went immediately to spend time with the children and parents. The worship pastor consulted with a few of us about changes to the worship service coming up in a couple of days. Someone else handled the phone calls coming in from newspapers, television, and eventually, national media. One of our pastors, traveling overseas at the time, diverted to Uganda to handle details and accompany the two caskets back home.

On the day of the funeral, more than two thousand people filed into our auditorium. The picture I will never get out of my mind at that funeral days later was the jarring sight of two dark-brown African mahogany caskets, side by side, with pictures of a forty-nine-year-old husband and a forty-nine-year-old wife all around.

What none of us knew at the time was that just weeks later we would get another shocking phone call. Michele was serving with the Wisconsin National Guard in Iraq when her Humvee came under attack. While she returned fire from her position in the vehicle, Michele was mortally wounded.

Before this, everybody in the city knew of Michele because there was media coverage when she, her twin sister, and her other sister all ended up getting deployed in Iraq. They had all been together in our worship service several months earlier when we prayed for the Wisconsin National Guard unit that was soon to be dispatched to the Middle East. All the newspapers in the region had carried a striking photo of the three sisters in their sand-colored fatigues, ready to depart.

Another earthquake in our community and in our church. Walking with a grief-stricken family, preparing for a difficult funeral. Responding to media from all over the country. Dealing with the insult of violent death. Every funeral following a tragic violent death is traumatic, but with the state governor and U.S. senators in attendance, this funeral showed the same dynamics written in capital letters.

I have a theory. A church's character and maturity can be directly measured by how it handles death, dying, and funerals. That line where we cross from this life to the life to come is the most defining moment as we try to understand the meaning and significance of our present lives.

An entirely different set of experiences take place when a church goes through a crisis of moral or ethical failure in one or more of its leaders. Whereas an untimely high-profile death produces a sudden grief, a crisis of an ethical or moral nature produces a sense of betrayal.

This story can be told many times over. A church is on a major upswing. It is growing. It is in the middle of a facilities expansion that the whole congregation is enthusiastic about. The pastor is as popular as he has ever been. In fact, his public image and that of his family is almost too good to be true. They come off as the perfect family. The pastor's name is known by people all over town. He is seen as a man of great vision, vigor, and courage. Then one day, completely out of the blue, the associate pastor and the chairman of the church's board show up at the church offices and gather the church staff for a special meeting. Their faces are sober, their words halting. The church's lead pastor has been immediately suspended pending an investigation of allegations of sexual misconduct with a woman in the church whom he had been counseling, and allegations that he had committed adultery with at least two other women earlier.

Incredulity and loyalty kick in immediately. Half the church's staff refuse to believe there is any possibility that the accusation is true, but the other half have a sick feeling that it may be. They have had a sense of unease with the pastor for some time. His words seemed right, but he had developed a plastic persona.

Initially the pastor vehemently denies the allegation, but within days two other women from the church come forward and tell of indiscretions that stretch back over five years. The pastor confesses. He and his family drop from sight. On Sunday, two representatives of the church's leadership deliver the news to the congregation, and an emotional associate pastor chokes out a shortened sermon.

But what happens next?

BEFORE CRISIS HITS: BUILDING A CHURCH TO WITHSTAND EARTHQUAKES

Jarring experiences test the Whole Church. Buildings that are constructed too stiffly will collapse in an earthquake; those that accept the reality of earthquakes will be built to withstand. So churches built on a stoic theology that considers any damage a lack of faith are living precariously. Expecting and being prepared for crisis is the only way to survive grief and trauma as a Whole Church. Here are some things you can do to build into a church the kind of strength and flexibility that will help it be ready for crises before they happen.

1.   Teach church leaders and the church in general to expect the unexpected. This is where building a church on solid biblical theology makes a difference. Death and moral failure are part and parcel of the human experience. Almost every page of Scripture shouts these harsh realities in our ears. Success is not our salvation. Image is not the same as reality. The more we think we are in control by our plans and programs, the higher our risk. We also risk missing some of the most important ministry we will engage in: responding with grace to people in crisis. Let's be honest. When we as leaders have our schedules all booked up with meetings and plans, we sometimes consider the unexpected tragedy an interruption. We need to be organized for the unexpected. If we (even subconsciously) think about crisis as an interruption to our flow of ministry, we will miss the best opportunity for ministry at the time.

2.   Accept that grief work is some of the most important work we do in the church. What is our highest agenda? Life and death. We proclaim and we teach that faith in Christ will carry a person over the line between life and death. The unexpected tragedy is an opportunity for the Whole Church to remember why it exists.

3.   Develop in church leaders a "minuteman" mentality. When church leaders and volunteers follow their better instincts to rise to the occasion when a tragedy happens, they realize that the church has this unique ability to respond quickly to human need. Responses may take the form of getting the church ready for a funeral, dealing with the media, organizing meals and other practical helps for a grieving family, or even organizing a ministry of mercy to a place where a natural disaster has occurred. In the case of other kinds of crisis, a broad base of leaders with a minuteman mentality will immediately organize prayer; they will gather in their small groups and talk through the issues, comforting each

other and keeping information clear (if there is already in place a reliable source of information from the church).

4.   Spread the task around. Tragedies take their toll on many circles of people. This is where the stronger members of the body can offset the weakness of some of the members. And at some other time, the roles will be reversed.

5.   Have plans for how to communicate during a rapidly unfolding crisis. Prepare the people who pick up the phone when the church number is called. Help grieving families decide who the spokesperson for the family should be. In the case of a sensitive development, a spokesperson needs to know what is public knowledge and what is confidential as the crisis unfolds. Speculation is deadly; putting a spin on a bad bit of news is equally destructive.

6.   In the case of a sudden dismissal of a pastor on a charge of something like sexual misconduct, the key leaders of the church need to get together and stay together, evaluating in a fair-minded way every twist and turn along the way. If the guilty party admits the sin, a proper process of spiritual care can unfold, but any attempt for quick restoration to leadership should be avoided. Forgiveness is one thing; qualifying for leadership is another. A pastor guilty of sexual misconduct may never be a pastor again.

7.   In the case of serious allegations of immorality, such as sexual misconduct, in which the pastor or other leader denies the accusation, the key leaders of the church (and maybe one or two other leaders from a different church) need to guide the church through the painful process of discovering the truth. The biblical concept that at least two or three witnesses are necessary to bring a charge against a leader is very important here. Consult with other churches that have weathered this storm. Be prepared for the congregation to have split loyalties.

IN PRACTICE—COHESIVE IDEAS FOR A WHOLE CHURCH

1. Get reliable information to the key church leaders immediately.
2. The key church leaders should designate a team of three to five people who will be the core responsible parties receiving new information and making a plan.
3. Commit to truthfulness in all matters, but do not assume that honesty means public disclosure of all information. Grieving families have rights. An unfolding potential moral crisis needs due process; people must be assumed innocent until proven guilty.
4. Know ahead of time what kind of crisis warrants contacting law enforcement authorities. When the law mandates notification, do not hesitate. Cooperate fully with the proper authorities.
5. Do not turn church leaders into detectives. Church leaders may need to make inquires, but they are ill-equipped for full-scale investigations of wrongdoing.
6. Draw in mature, respected leaders from other churches if there is a protracted conflict over moral accusations.
7. Give the church receptionist or whoever answers the phone a proper set of information to give people when they call the church. Keep the information updated.
8. Do not spread speculation. (In the case of the murdered missionaries described earlier, everyone wanted to know what group was responsible for the killing. Was it thugs? Military militia? Religious extremists? No one knew for sure—and that remained the case for months. The only right answer to the question "Who did this?" was "We really don't know at this point.")
9. Help the congregation at an emotional level by acknowledging the loss brought about by the crisis. Do not launch into artificial stoicism.
10. At the same time, demonstrate the strength that comes from faith in God in the midst of the crisis.

11. Use Scripture as a foundation for people to stand on in a time of crisis.
12. Be ready to have a special church meeting if a significant crisis breaks. This can be a time when relevant information is passed along, but it may not be a time for open questions and answers if the situation is unfolding.
13. In any special church meeting called in the midst of a crisis, keep prayer the highest priority.
14. Recruit a care team to meet the needs of families immediately affected by a major crisis.
15. Have an emergency plan in case something happens and the church building cannot be occupied for a time.
16. Train small groups in the church to be a first line of prayer for any crisis that might erupt. This further solidifies the purpose of small groups as a fundamental structure for the church.
17. Have some funds set aside in the church budget to be able to meet emergency needs in a crisis.
18. Before a crisis erupts, establish a church policy about fundraising for families going through a crisis. Letting people know where gifts can be contributed to a needy family is one thing, but be careful about setting a precedent with regard to fundraisers for needy individuals, because the church will have to be consistent with whatever that policy is in the future.
19. Don't set artificial timetables for how long the church will grieve. Every situation is different.
20. Don't assume anything about "closure." The very idea may be artificial—just ask people who have lost a child. They will tell you that there is no such thing as closure.
21. Teach that grief may hurt, but does not injure.
22. Teach that the calling of the church to be a place of refuge, comfort, and healing is one of its highest callings.
23. Train church leaders in how to be responsive in times of tragedy.
24. Make hospital visitation a high priority for someone in leadership.
25. Keep helpful literature on hand for grieving people.

12

FAILURES AND SUCCESSES IN COMMUNICATION

THE BIG IDEA
Problems in communication are the roots of many episodes of fragmentation in a church, but when leaders place a high priority on communication and execute it well, congregations are much more likely to experience "the shared life."

I can't prove it, and I can't quantify it, but on the basis of my experience of going through hundreds of problems of fragmentation in the church, I believe that the vast majority of the time (90 percent? 95 percent?), there is some failure in communication that makes a problem worse or is the start of the problem in the first place.

But let's not start this chapter on an entirely negative note. To set the topic positively: when the Whole Church is operating in the very best way, the grace and the truth of Christ flow freely within the church and to spiritually desperate people outside the church through effective and substantial communication. But before we proceed, please set aside the assumption that communication is merely the transmission of information. Communication is, in its full sense, the transmission of life.

COMMUNICATION AND THE SHARED LIFE

The word *communication* comes from a Latin root meaning "to share." This ties in nicely to the biblical ideal of *koinonia*, fellowship, which is "the shared life" (see Chapter Six). The aim of communication within the church and outside it should be the shared life. It is not just about passing on information about what programs meet on what days and in what rooms—although communication as the shared life certainly includes the clear transmission of information. Communication is not just about letting people know of changes that will affect them—although it includes that, too. Good communication in the church includes the facts and the figures, the whys, wheres, and what-fors—but it goes on to link people with people, lives with lives. Communication is the means by which human beings connect with other human beings. Communication is about knowing people, knowing the heart of the leaders, knowing the pain and struggles of people, knowing the vision, knowing each other's successes, and knowing the failures, too. Communication is the ligaments and sinews that hold a body together. Or you can think of communication as the circulatory system of a body. The blood vessels large and small are the passageway enabling life-giving, oxygen-enriched blood to get to every bit of tissue in every part of the body. Cut off the blood, however (choke the communication), and the body's tissues die.

Because communication is such a make-or-break issue for any church, I ask leaders from other churches about their successes and failures in communication all the time. I suppose I've asked dozens of leaders in different churches about how they feel they are doing in the area of communication, and I'm always amazed at the responses I get. I've talked to the leaders of some of the best-known churches in the country, and what I hear from them and from everyone else is this: *they are not at all satisfied with how they are doing with communication.*

Now that could be very discouraging, or it could simply be one more indication of how important and complicated communication is. Put it another way: if we ever catch ourselves feeling entirely satisfied with our communication, we probably have settled for something that is less than what God has called us to. We should not be afraid of our dissatisfaction with communication; it is our best indicator that we realize how important the shared life is.

COMMUNICATION, MOTIVE, AND TRUST

When any of us as leaders are honest with ourselves and with God, we know that behind the issue of communication looms a value question: the issue of motive. So let's start there. Every leader has to ask himself or herself, *Is my motive in* what *I communicate and* how *I communicate in my church an honest description of what is true?*

The highest currency in any church community is trust. And the way trust is earned is through decent motives, reflected in honest communication. What this means is that when a congregation hears something from its leaders, it knows that what the leaders are saying is not spin, not slyness, and certainly not deception. The congregation knows that truth and honesty are at the top of the church leadership's list of values, so when it hears a message from the leadership, it trusts that there is no ulterior motive or hidden agenda behind the words. Adopt that stance for a long time (years or decades), and congregation and leaders build up a trust relationship that becomes the backbone of the church.

But what does honesty mean? Every church leader on the inside track knows that there are scores of situations that ought *not* to become matters of public information. There are matters of personal confidentiality that require discretion. In the normal course of ministry, pastors hear about circumstances that warrant (and oftentimes require) clergy confidentiality. There are other matters that should be dealt with among the circle of people directly affected (perhaps pastors and governing board), and these matters are not best served by becoming matters of public consumption. Honesty does not mean that everybody knows everything at all times. It means that a leader is willing to sacrifice personal pride enough to be open about any issue on any day—*with the people who are in the need-to-know circle.* Okay, there's the tricky part. Some leaders will make the mistake of assuming that hardly anybody is on a need-to-know status on a given issue, and that is to be too restrictive. There are other leaders who feel that they are not being honest unless they satisfy the people in a congregation who believe that they are always within the need-to-know circle. Let's face it: we're up against human nature here. Everybody wants to believe that he or she is in the inner circle, and everybody who has something delicate going on wants to limit the number of people drawn into the inner circle. Leaders who are honest and who engender trust in a congregation are mature and discerning about who needs to know what, but are always truthful in what is actually said. (And in my experience, the most mature people understand that discretion is part of honest communication.)

Here are some principles that may help govern the "need-to-know" issue:

1.   The scriptural principle of "speaking the truth in love" truly does bind us to the truth, but protects us by binding us simultaneously to a motive of doing what is responsible and helpful for the people we serve. Love is not an add-on; it is to be the quality and character of how we communicate.

2.   Communication needs to minimize or even exclude the possibility of gossip, which is described in numerous biblical passages as a substantial sin (though, to our shame, in the church we give ourselves implicit permission to gossip in all different ways).

3.   Any leader and, in particular, the main leader of a church should not hesitate to admit that he or she is a flawed and fallible human being, along with everyone else. This is not accomplished necessarily by making startling admissions of failure (confession always needs to be done with the circle appropriate to the offense), but by adopting a steady attitude of humility and teachability and a deferential stance toward the congregation and other leaders.

4.   When leaders deal with scandalous or incendiary matters that come up in the congregation, they need to form an appropriate circle of people to deal with the issue forthrightly and honestly, but with discretion.

COMMUNICATION AND THE SPIRIT OF A CHURCH

The highest accomplishment of any church cannot be measured by numbers or even described in a bullet-point list of goals achieved. Look at the words of Jesus to the seven churches in the opening chapters of Revelation, and you see that what are celebrated in churches are accomplishments of character.

One of the things that have always been the greatest encouragements to me as a pastor is hearing from newcomers that they have been profoundly moved, although they find the source of the feeling hard to describe. It's not just that they heard great music or a moving message. Not just that the greeters were friendly toward them or that the signage in the building helped them find the wing where their kids' classrooms are. It is that there is something different here. A different kind of spirit. A feeling of coming to life. It is these kinds of clues that sometimes tell us that God is at work in people's lives, and that God is working to develop a spirit in a church that is itself an act of grace for people looking to find a place of peace.

The spirit of a church is something very hard to define or describe, but may be one of the most important things we communicate. Yes, people like it when they get the information they need, but far more important to them is that they get the hope they need. Communication is the shared life, not just shared information.

So when a pastor or someone else gives a few announcements in a worship service, he or she needs to remember that as important as the information is, what he or she says about the values and the spirit of the church is even more important.

For instance, someone can give the following announcement:

Our giving for the first six months of the year is 5 percent less than our budgeted goals. There will be stresses and strains in our ministry and staff if we don't hit 100 percent. So let's all see if we can dig deep and catch up to the 100 percent mark.

Or that person can say,

We're halfway through the year, and God has enabled us to do some great things in ministry within our church family and in outreach. Your financial gifts have made so much of this possible. Our giving, as of right now, is at 95 percent of our goals, so let's see what we can do to recommit ourselves to the mission as the second half of the year unfolds. As always, your giving is an act of worship and is confidential between you and God—but if each of us does what God calls us to do, there is no doubt that we will get up to 100 percent of our goals, and even surpass any goals any of us envision.

One thing that church members deeply appreciate is being respected. Talking down to them, "spinning" a message, obfuscating the truth, or manipulating them with emotion always loses more ground than it gains. People are smart. If we treat them as if they were brainless, they will think we are brainless ourselves, or (worst yet) they will go along with it and respond in a brainless way and reinforce a culture of churchy imbecility. Church leaders can develop (or may even want to develop) congregations moved by whim or sentiment, but does anybody think that such churches will be agents of transformation in their communities?

The spirit of a church is the collective values that have been reinforced over the years. Care for people, awe before God, humility regarding reputation, compassion for the lost, respect for the senior citizen and adolescent, enthusiasm for racial and ethnic diversity in the church, sympathy for the outcast—these are the kinds of values that can be fostered in a congregation, and can be at the core of communication at all times. This is what will tell people why a church exists, and why they should care that it exists. This is why we communicate.

COMMUNICATING INFORMATION

Communication as the shared life is not limited to the imparting of information, but it does include information. People in a church will feel well cared for when its leaders are responsible in ensuring that relevant and fresh information keeps coming to them at all times. Here are some of the essentials in effective communication of information:

1. Decide what the major organs for communicating information will be, and shape the congregation's expectations accordingly. Will you choose to use a weekly bulletin handed out in the worship service? A monthly newsletter? A weekly e-mail to all church members? (You will need to know what percentage of people in your church use e-mail.) The church's Web site? Word of mouth (often the most effective, and most underutilized)? A combination or all of the above? Whether we like it or not (and I know I don't like it because it seems insulting and a waste of energy), communication requires much repetition. The communicator may feel that putting an announcement in the bulletin or a one-time all-church e-mail does the trick, but in this day and age, people are used to getting messages sent to them multiple times (advertising being the key example). People may first "hear"

a message the third time it is given to them. This is one reason why we have to be selective in choosing our key messages.

2.   Change your way of thinking about communication from top-down to bottom-up. Most church leaders have an extremely difficult time understanding this or being willing to act on it. In our role as leaders, our default position always is to focus on the messages *we* want to communicate and that *we* believe the congregation needs to know. Reasonable, right? Well, yes and no. Effective communication is cyclical. Leaders create messages that they seek to promulgate within the church, but leaders also need to do the hard work of understanding what information a congregation *wants* to know. Just pause there. Ask if you are willing to do that work.

3.   Revise your church's means of communication every couple of years. Don't be timid about getting rid of tools that don't work. Take a fresh look.

4.   Continually search for truly creative people in the church. Creative people who understand the philosophy, life, and history of the church are invaluable. But they also must have the right attitude, be ready to be recruited as writers or artists for projects, and willing to revise and adapt.

COMMUNICATING CHANGE

Changes in themselves are challenging enough for a church, but if changes are poorly communicated, they become opportunities for serious fragmentation or loss of good will.

Let's say your church is going to change worship service times, rearrange the children's ministry program, and add a new outreach-type service on Saturday night. Or imagine that the church's leaders believe it is time to move toward a major capital campaign. Some significant kind of change. The wrong way to approach communicating these changes is to assume that the leaders' decision on the matter is sacrosanct and that at the right time information will be given to the congregation so that they'll know when to go where. This would be to miss the spiritual dynamics of change, the need for ownership, and the opportunity for the changes to be a motivational development.

The best way to approach communicating a significant change involves planning and work, and the dividends are enormous.

1.   Make a plan! There is some improvisation in communication, but it always works best when planned. A communication plan for most projects can be outlined on one or two pieces of paper. At a glance you can see if you have a balance of verbal, print, e-mail, Web site, and word-of-mouth communication. You can also plan the timing of the messages as they reflect developments in the situation. Without a plan, most communication about a significant initiative of a church becomes reactive and tardy. Reacting to frustration should not be the default mode of communication.

2.   Give hints to the congregation that changes are being contemplated (for instance, changing worship times, adding a service, or changing children's programming) before the decision is finally made. This gives people a chance to chime in early (just expect that the most vocal will be people whose knee-jerk reaction will be not to like the idea).

3.   Respect the people centrally involved (for example, key leaders) by keeping them informed of the decision-making process at each step.

4.   Many weeks before a large change, communicate to the congregation what the changes will be and, just as important, *why* they are being made. Judge the right moment to put a printed piece in everybody's hand that will describe all the elements of the change, clearly highlighting the practical details people need to know. Let them know that this is their reference guide for all the details. Use verbal communication to highlight the important messages, but don't count on the verbal to impart information.

5.   Don't stop communicating after the change. Congratulate those who made it possible. Congratulate the congregation for moving through the change. Don't focus on the small number of people who may have complained vociferously.

IN PRACTICE—COHESIVE IDEAS FOR A WHOLE CHURCH

1. Revolutionize your thinking about communication. Think bottom-up. Let the questions and concerns of the congregation be at least as relevant as the message that leaders from the top down want to get across.
2. Teach all leaders that communication is an act of grace and love, not one of manipulating people. Communication is the way shepherds guide the flock toward life.
3. Evaluate the tools of communication you are using now by surveying the congregation or conducting a couple of focus groups. Learn lessons from what is working, and give up all assumptions about what you think should work.
4. Even though Internet Web sites are a major focus of communication in churches today, don't give up on having one main printed piece that is the key reference point for the Whole Church. There is no substitute for the tangible.
5. Make sure that the main printed piece (for example, a weekly item) highlights two or three main messages. Many (if not most) church attenders will just notice the headlines of our communications.
6. Keep your expectations reasonable. If only 25 percent of the people read a printed piece, that is not a failure—you have accomplished something significant by getting that many people to listen to a message. Think about the magazines or newspapers you subscribe to—how much of them do you read?
7. When there is a major issue needing understanding, produce a stand-alone piece that explains the issue in detail, with carefully crafted words. This approach is appropriate when you're trying to explain, for example, the rationale for a building project, a change in direction in the church, or a revision of the constitution.
8. If your church doesn't have a Web site, create one. It does not have to be fancy or elaborate or expensive. People are rapidly developing a mind-set that any responsible organization will have essential information on the Web.

 9. Approach the Web site from the standpoint of the user. A simple, clear, user-friendly interface will help people the most, and they will appreciate it.
10. Use the Web site as an outreach tool. Some churches have two main sections on their Web site—one for church members and the other for the general public. The possibilities of helping unchurched people are tremendous.
11. Use verbal communication to emphasize major messages (in the worship service, for instance, or at another time when the whole congregation is gathered), but don't rely on it for information. Information given verbally often goes in one ear and out the other. And people will assume that if the message is important, it will come to them in print form anyway.
12. If you are a teaching pastor, embed important congregational messages in the teaching of the worship service. Church life issues are some of the best illustrations we can use.
13. Continually ask individuals what means of communication are working for them.
14. Investigate what broadcast media in your area are willing to make public service announcements at a time when your church is involved in a service to the community. (Don't expect any media to give free generic advertising to your church.)
15. If you are contacted by local media for an interview on some breaking news story, accept the opportunity unless you have reason to believe that the subject of the interview or the attitude of the interviewer is cynical.
16. When doing media interviews, prepare ahead of time the main messages you'd want to communicate. In interviews, take your time in speaking. Anything you can say may be quoted, and if you say something cavalier or flip or careless, that is likely to get quoted.
17. Every year try some new form of communication that you haven't before (print, Internet, verbal, advertising).
18. If you have any media or advertising professionals in your church, get their advice on how the church is doing in communication. But make sure they are well versed in the culture and values of your church.
19. Develop an all-church e-mail list, and use it sparingly so that what you send does not seem like junk mail to church members.

20. Assume that individual ministries will develop their own internal e-mail lists. It may be helpful to guide these communicators in the best techniques for using e-mail with a specific subgroup, but don't flatten personality or initiative.
21. Letters matter to people. An occasional printed letter from the main leader of the church mailed to people's homes will be read. If a message is brief, use a half-page format. Be radically concise.
22. Use your church's Web site not just for information about meetings but as an ever-expanding resource for quality spiritual growth material. You may post resources from other sites if you get permission, and making links is always possible.
23. Develop a communications team (volunteers in some churches, staff in others). Be sure that you have covered the functions of creativity and project management.
24. Develop a volunteer or staff role for director of communications.
25. Focus, focus, focus on the main message at any one time in your church.

13

CHOOSING WISE LEADERS

THE BIG IDEA
A Whole Church is held together by the stable perspectives of leaders gifted with wisdom. For some reason, we don't talk much about wisdom in church leadership, but if we would, we would set ourselves on a course of responsible, steady leadership.

Among the most common buzzwords associated with leadership in the church today are *passion* and *vision*. But another characteristic of quality leadership that is a nonnegotiable, one that we neglect at our own peril, is wisdom.

A leader can have passion enough to make listeners almost swoon and can pass on a contagious zeal, but if people are not moved into paths carefully defined by wisdom, then the result may be dramatic movement without anybody really going anywhere.

So too may a leader cast a great vision, imparting images of what may be, and even a new way of seeing, but if the vision is not defined and focused by wisdom, then the leader may be leading people toward what merely *could* be, rather than what *should* be.

WHY WISDOM MATTERS

In the best of circumstances, leaders let the "wisdom from above" point their eyes in the right direction to gain vision and to keep their passion pushing at the proper pace.

Why then is it that in discussions about leadership, wisdom gets relatively little attention? Let's face it: wisdom is not one of our flashier concepts. It conjures up pictures of owls—up high and aloof, mysterious, and oh so stationary. We think of wisdom as the special property of the elderly and wizened. And to these misconceptions we add this: we treat wisdom as some kind of treasury stored up in a few people's souls that ordinary folks draw on when it's really needed. In this view, wisdom is the exception rather than the rule. It is the belief that there are leaders and then there are really wise leaders, the kind every church should have in reserve—when they're really needed.

But Scripture does not allow us to ghettoize the wise, nor to cast wisdom itself as a rare gem. Wisdom is God's normal gift for ordinary times, and it is at the core of good leadership.

For years now, whenever our church's council of elders sets about the task of selecting new elders, I've given my one standard plea: please, oh please, find candidates who are wise. The discussions about whether a particular person would be a good elder easily gravitate toward the standard questions: Is he a godly person? What is his reputation? Are his gifts a good match for the needs of this assignment? But if we can use all these typical, appropriate filters and also ask, Does this person have wisdom? then we will end up with the kind of leader who will have a long-lasting and deep influence in the church. Zeal adds spark, and devotion adds shine, but wisdom in leadership yields substance and stability.

The most responsible leaders will cherish wisdom, as was the case with Joshua, who couldn't possibly have done what he needed to do without the "spirit of wisdom" that rested on him. Solomon's wisest word was his request for wisdom in order to lead: "Give me wisdom and knowledge, that I may lead this people." In Proverbs 8, wisdom has a voice of its own: not a whisper or a secret, but a shout and a call: "To you, O men, I call out; I raise my voice to all mankind. You who are simple, gain prudence; you who are foolish, gain understanding. Listen, for I have worthy things to say; I open my lips to speak what is right" (8:4–6). In Proverbs, to be wise is to be discerning, humble, prudent, fair, and right. What a blessing when we find those things in ourselves or in the leaders we work with: discernment with which to see the differences between major and minor issues; humility so that we don't make ourselves the issue; prudence, which not only judges what is right but predicts different contingencies; fairness and rightness, which cause others to trust and to want to follow.

Human nature does not naturally submit to wisdom. As Abba Eban, the Israeli politician, said, "History teaches us that men and nations behave wisely once they have exhausted all other alternatives."[1] Have you ever seen that in the church? We apply every other test to a challenging decision, and then the wise person in the room shows that discernment, humility, prudence, fairness, and rightness point in a clear direction. It may not be the easiest course, or the fanciest, but it is the best.

James speaks of the "wisdom from above" as the antithesis of envy and selfish ambition, which can only produce "disorder and every evil practice" (3:16). Wisdom from heaven (3:17) is . . .

"first of all pure" (wise people have godly motives)

"then peace-loving" (wise people value the Whole Church; they are disturbed by conflict)

"considerate" (wise people are emotionally intelligent, and care about others)

"submissive" (wise people consider others better than themselves)

"full of mercy and good fruit" (wise people do real acts of mercy)

"impartial" (wise people give a fair hearing to all sides)

" sincere" (wise people are honest in what they say and how they act)

To be wise, in other words, is more than being smart. You can be the most intelligent person in the world and be a fool. Wisdom means to be good and, in so doing, to be right. When leaders make wise decisions, the people who have their eyes open will nod their heads in knowing assent because they see behind those decisions the attitudes of generosity, selflessness, fairness, and rightness. Wisdom gives people reason to trust.

The question of the day is, How do we find wise leaders? It would be a simple thing if one only needed to look for white hair. But age alone does not impart wisdom (remember the aphorism: "older, but no wiser").

SEVEN CHARACTERISTICS TO LOOK FOR IN FINDING WISE LEADERS

Let's address the question of how to find wise leaders by way of a hypothetical situation. It is time to appoint a new leader: a new board member, a chairman of a building committee, or a new pastor. How do we know when we are looking at someone who has wisdom? On the basis of biblical criteria and common experience, we could ask these seven questions.[2]

1. *Does this person show evidence of grace through a generosity of spirit, a love for mercy, an ability to forgive?* Wise spiritual leaders have a vision of God's great flow of grace to us and through us. They see the power of grace as one of the fundamental realities of life: that God creates and re-creates, all out of his relentless love. Thus wisdom dictates that we go with that flow and that the decisions that we make in the church about programs and people and budgets must cooperate with that great divine work of grace. This is why James warns about people (and, we may add, leaders) who are motivated by envy and selfish ambition. These are the attitudes and motives that are completely out of touch with God's grace-work. Sometimes ambitious people are appointed as leaders just because they are ambitious. They are willing to step in where others are not. In such cases, oftentimes, wisdom doesn't have a chance because the leader is looking more to get than to give.

2. *Does this person have a good reputation with others? Is he or she the kind of person others seek out for advice and support?* People who are wise are a treasure to those around them. They say things that stick for a long time because wise words go deep into the heart of any issue. They influence by planting seeds in people's minds and hearts, which over the long haul show fruit. People with wisdom are trusted by others because it is clear that they are more interested in knowing God than impressing people. They realize how ridiculous self-interest is. Wise people are honest. There is integrity (which means wholeness) in what they stand for.

3. *Does this person live a consistent life?* Where there is wisdom, there is stability. Please do not read "consistent" or "stable" as dull

or mediocre. This is not about intensity or flair or the lack thereof. We need leaders who are consistent and stable in that their personal lives and their public lives are congruent. There needs to be an integrity or wholeness to who they are, what they think, and how they act. Wise people do not get sucked into the latest fad. They can be enthusiastic about a novel idea, but they are patient enough to let time tell whether something has a shelf life of a year or a decade, or whether it is something that has enduring value. Wisdom prevents people from swinging from one intense commitment to another. Wise people do not leave one bridge after another half built. They do not leave their followers as orphans.

4.   *Does this person show a reasonable breadth of thought?* Wise people know what they believe, and they are intensely committed to it, but they also want to be able to understand divergent points of view, and they are open to adapting their thinking because they are wise enough to know that they don't know everything. Wise people know what the nonnegotiables are, as opposed to the minor issues. In discussions about worship, evangelism, youth ministry, facilities, and almost anything else, wise leaders know the difference between issues of style and those of substance. But how do they know the difference? Again, this knowledge arises out of spiritual character. Wisdom dictates that we do not selfishly promote our preferences. It prevents us from feeling threatened by a new idea. Wisdom requires us to be open to many ideas, yet it frees us from feeling pushed and pulled by the rush of the day. It is also our only hope that we will be lifelong learners in the school of Christ. When we are wise, we freely admit how often we succumb to foolishness.

5.   *Does this person show a depth of thought?* Wise leaders look beneath the surface of the issues they face. They want their decisions to be based on principles, and this takes some mental and spiritual effort. Behind every program decision in a church, there is a why (the principle), and behind every principle there is a why (which is a matter of values). Our values are the why behind the why. And values can be developed only with the use of wisdom.

6. *Would other people describe this person as fair-minded?* Leaders have to be impartial. Their judgments about matters will engender trust only if people see that the judgments don't waver from one situation to the next. Little children are quick to say, "But that's not fair!" because sensitivity to justice is core to our existence. We need it; we count on it. Churches are communities of people looking for models of fairness and justice.

7. *Has this person learned some lessons in life through hard times?* Some of the deepest wisdom follows from deep pain. Suffering strips us down to the bare essentials; it puts in perspective the things that really matter in life; it teaches us the things that belong to the soul. Pain humbles us and forces us to find the true foundations for life. Remember the adage "sadder, but wiser." Ecclesiastes puts it this way: "Sorrow is better than laughter, because a sad face is good for the heart. The heart of the wise is in the house of mourning, but the heart of fools is in the house of pleasure" (7:3–4). This is not a gloomy invitation for us to live a dour life. Rather, it means that when hard times come, it is best to face them honestly, go through grief with integrity, and come out wiser for it. In leadership, that wisdom will be like gold someday.

DON'T GIVE UP ON LOOKING FOR WISE LEADERS

If you are thinking now, "I don't know if I know anybody in my church (myself included!) who would meet all these criteria!" then you're certainly not alone. Please do not take these questions in an absolute way. They are markers. Any wisdom that we do find in ourselves or other leaders is a work in progress. One thing that we should be absolutely clear about: we should never assign leadership roles to people who would be described in Proverbs as fools. It is not unkind to say that if a person is imprudent, self-absorbed, unmerciful, or partial, he or she will not be assigned a leadership role. It doesn't matter if that person is the only one willing to chair the board or the building committee or if that person has the most passion and zeal. If he or she shows a complete lack of wisdom, then someone else should be given the assignment. Alarm bells should go off if someone suggested as a leader can't take criticism, can't seem to problem-solve, and seems to be continually surrounded by crisis or chaos.

Wisdom is a free-flowing gift of God. There is not a group of people who have a corner on God's wisdom, people who are wise all the time in every circumstance. And it is possible for wisdom to come from almost anybody, any time. But insofar as we can be looking for leaders who, even in youth, show an affinity for "the wisdom from above," we will have our best chance at ministry that has quality and integrity.

- -
IN PRACTICE—COHESIVE IDEAS
FOR A WHOLE CHURCH
- -

1. Do your own biblical study of "the wisdom from above" in James 3.
2. Read through the book of Proverbs and make a list of all the characteristics of the wise person and the characteristics of the fool.
3. Find a time to talk with your fellow leaders about the subject of this chapter: What does "wisdom from heaven" look like in your ministry?
4. Talk with fellow leaders about the people in your church in the past who have been pillars of wisdom.
5. Find a way for people of wisdom to have a voice in your leadership.
6. Oftentimes people with wisdom are sitting on the sidelines, or they have had their day in leadership. Don't ignore them. Seek out their wisdom.
7. If you do testimonials in your worship services, make sure you often let wise people voice their perspectives.
8. When your church is coming up on major changes, consult with known wise people to get their perspective.
9. Be aware that although wise people's voices must be listened to, it is only natural that if these individuals are of an older generation, they may be very cautious or even overly cautious when it comes to change.

10. When changes are taking place, let the conspicuously wise people be a significant influence for the congregation.
11. For any and all pivotal leadership roles (pastors, board members), do not settle for anything less than wisdom as an essential characteristic.
12. Look for wisdom in young people. The gift of wisdom is not limited by age, but it is seasoned by age.
13. As a leader, seek out your own circle of wise counselors who will honestly guide you.
14. Tell wise people you trust that they should feel free at any time to give you a word of wisdom, whether it is one of encouragement, warning, guidance, or correction.
15. Ask God to give you, as a leader, the gift of wisdom. Remember God's response when Solomon asked for wisdom (study 1 Kings 3–4).
16. Remember that wisdom does not make anyone immune from sin. Wise Solomon became arrogant Solomon.
17. When appointing someone to head a major committee (such as a building committee), don't just look at practical qualifications but at the spiritual qualification of wisdom.
18. When hiring a youth pastor or other worker, use the "wisdom from heaven" (James 3:17) filter. That staff person's influence on kids will be directly related to his or her wisdom.
19. Reward accomplishments of wisdom in leadership, not just ambition and passion.
20. Discover three authors who have extraordinary insight into human nature; over time, read several of their books.
21. Use the values of wisdom to shape your church's priorities, vision, and program.
22. Tell the stories of believers who made wise decisions at crucial turning points in the life of their families or in their work.
23. Put this verse on your desk, and make it a daily prayer: "The wisdom that comes from heaven is first of all pure; then peace-loving, considerate, submissive, full of mercy and good fruit, impartial and sincere" (James 3:17).
24. When giving counsel to others, ask God to help you offer them sincere wisdom.
25. Imagine that this year is your last in ministry. What do you need to do in this time for people to be able to say, "He [or she] was a wise leader"?

AFTERWORD

As I've worked on this book over the past couple of years I have tried to imagine you, the reader, the whole way through—and that is not hard to do. Whether you are a pastor in a small or large church, or a church board member, or a seminary student—wherever you live and however long you've been doing church ministry—you and I know that the ministry of the local church is a high calling entrusted to us all-too-human leaders.

Whole Church isn't just an idea or a theory. It is what we all want. Just like the Hebrew greeting "shalom," which means, "may you be healthy, may you be blessed, may you be *whole*," isn't that what we all want and what we want for each other? God help us if we don't want it.

Whole Church is a call for twenty-first-century church leaders. A high calling. People who need the saving grace of Jesus Christ are searching for a power of reconciliation—something or someone who pulls life together, a truly cohesive dynamic of life. These people feel like their lives are being pulled apart, torn apart, split apart, falling apart. They are ordinary people living with ordinary gaps (just as we leaders are). They need the God who makes all things whole. But why should they believe that is possible if the church is content to leave fractures, contradictions, and gaps unattended.

Whole Church is at one and the same time an impossible goal, but the only one worth aiming at.

We need to give up empty rhetoric about unity. When we talk about unity, it needs to be with longing, aching, and real hope. And we need to get practical. We need to "Make every effort to keep the unity of the Spirit through the bond of peace" (Eph. 4:3). "Every effort" includes our preaching, our planning, our communications, our worship, our administration, our teaching. In the church we live with this paradox—almost anything we do can be the source of disagreement and division, or it can be a God-inhabited experience of cohesion.

Don't give up. Be glad for every experience of wholeness you have. Don't discard people who disagree with you. That's not wholeness. Seek to bridge the gaps, to carry out "the ministry of reconciliation." And be encouraged in this: it is the energy of the reconciling God that makes all this possible.

You may have heard the story of the speech Winston Churchill gave at a school assembly long after he had retired from politics. It is said he strode to the rostrum and said these words: "Never give up. Never, ever, ever, ever give up." And then he took his seat.

Great leaders persevere because they know they are called to a great mission.

* * *

For more practical help: www.wholechurch.org

NOTES

CHAPTER ONE

1. See the discussion and study helps for leader groups at www.wholechurch.org.

CHAPTER TWO

1. Unless otherwise indicated, all survey information in this chapter comes from "Insights into Congregational Conflict," written by Carl Dudley, Theresa Zingery, and David Breeden for Faith Communities Today, a nonprofit wing of Hartford Seminary and the Hartford Institute for Religion Research.

2. Survey conducted by Christianity Today, Inc., and reported in *Your Church,* Nov.-Dec. 2005 and Jan.-Feb. 2006.

CHAPTER THREE

1. See www.wholechurch.org for supplemental teaching resources.

2. See presentation resources at www.wholechurch.org.

CHAPTER FOUR

1. Churches and their leaders will use different terms: preaching, teaching, speaking. I am referring here to the ministry of the Word, no matter whether there is a pulpit, a music stand, or nothing; no matter whether it is to a church of two thousand or of twenty.

2. A case in point: a sermon series at Elmbrook Church based on 1 Corinthians but responding to survey questions from the congregation. The series was called "The Questions We Ask."

3. See examples of long and short sermon series at www.whole-church.org.

4. For instance, Philip Yancey, *Prayer: Does It Make Any Difference?* (Grand Rapids, Mich.: Zondervan, 2006).

CHAPTER FIVE

1. Robert Wuthnow, *Sharing the Journey: Support Groups and America's New Quest for Community* (New York: Free Press, 1994).

2. Two of the newest books are Larry Osborne, *Sticky Church* (Grand Rapids, Mich.: Zondervan, 2008), and Bill Search, *Simple Small Groups* (Grand Rapids, Mich.: Baker, 2008).

3. For more information on these kinds of programs, go to www.elmbrook.org.

CHAPTER SEVEN

1. An Internet search on "faith promise" will yield many churches' practices and variations.

CHAPTER EIGHT

1. For more information, see Mel Lawrenz, *Jubilee: Enter a Season of Spiritual Renewal* (Ventura, Calif.: Regal Books, 2008).

CHAPTER NINE

1. See Mel Lawrenz, *Patterns: Ways to Develop a God-Filled Life* (Grand Rapids, Mich.: Zondervan, 2003).

2. At Elmbrook Church this has taken the form of a "First Friday Fellowship" for the morning and lunch hour, which features special speakers who offer substantial teaching. On the other three Fridays of the month, the church offers seminars and small group growth opportunities.

CHAPTER THIRTEEN

1. As quoted in the *Times* [of London], Dec. 17, 1970, from a speech given in London, Dec. 16, 1970; and in Alfred J. Kolatch, *Great Jewish Quotations* (Flushing, N.Y.: Jonathan David, 1996), p. 115.

2. This list first appeared in *Leadership,* Spring 2002.

THE AUTHOR

Mel Lawrenz has been a pastor in churches small and large, denominational and nondenominational. For the past twenty-nine years, he has been a pastor at Elmbrook Church in Brookfield, Wisconsin, succeeding Stuart Briscoe as senior pastor eight years ago. Elmbrook Church is an evangelical nondenominational church with an average attendance of six thousand and a long-standing global outreach.

Mel has written numerous books for leadership and general audiences. His passion for the ministry of the written word has opened an international audience through the Internet. He also has a broadcast ministry on radio and online, Faith Conversations (www.cometothebrook.org).

Mel studied writing at Carroll College (B.A.), and he holds an M.Div. from Trinity Evangelical Divinity School and a Ph.D. in historical theology (early church) from Marquette University.

Mel and his wife of thirty-four years, Ingrid, have lived in various locations around Lake Michigan, from the beauty of Door County to the rush of Chicago. They have a son and daughter, both in college.

Mel's personal interests include almost anything that will get him outdoors, particularly if it's near a body of water.

INDEX

Missional Renaissance

Changing the Scorecard for the Church

Reggie McNeal

Hardcover
ISBN: 978-0-470-24344-2

"Any new book by Reggie McNeal is something of an event, and this book is no exception. Not only is this an excellent introduction to missional Christianity, but it establishes a much-needed metric by which we can assess the vitality of this highly significant new movement."

—Alan Hirsch, author, *The Forgotten Ways*, *Rejesus*, and *The Shaping of Things to Come*; founding director, Forge Mission Training System; co-founder, shapevine.com

Missional Renaissance is McNeal's much-anticipated follow-up to his groundbreaking, best-selling book, *The Present Future,* which quickly became one of the definitive works on the "missional church movement."

In *Missional Renaissance*, Reggie McNeal shows the three significant shifts in the church leaders' thinking and behavior that will allow their congregations to chart a course toward becoming truly a missional congregation. To embrace the missional model, church leaders and members must shift from an internal to an external focus, ending the church as exclusive social club model, from running programs and ministries to developing people as its core activity, and from church-based leadership to community-engaged leadership.

The book is filled with in-depth discussions of what it means to become a missional congregation and important information on how to make the transition. *Missional Renaissance* offers a clear path for any leader or congregation that wants to breathe new life into the church and to become revitalized as true followers of Jesus.

REGGIE MCNEAL serves as the Missional Leadership Specialist for Leadership Network of Dallas, Texas. McNeal is the author of *A Work of Heart: Understanding How God Shapes Spiritual Leaders*, the best-selling *The Present Future: Six Tough Questions for the Church*, and *Practicing Greatness: 7 Disciplines of Extraordinary Spiritual Leaders* from Jossey-Bass. To learn more, visit **www.missionalrenaissance.org.**

The Present Future
Six Tough Questions for the Church

REGGIE MCNEAL

Paperback
ISBN: 978-0-470-45315-5

NOW AVAILABLE IN PAPERBACK!

"This is the most courageous book I have ever read on church life. McNeal nails the problem on the head. Be prepared to be turned upside down and shaken loose of all your old notions of what church is and should be in today's world."

—**George Cladis**, senior pastor, Westminster Presbyterian Church, Oklahoma City, Oklahoma and author, _Leading the Team-Based Church_

In _The Present Future_, author, consultant, and church leadership developer Reggie McNeal debunks old assumptions about church leadership and provides an overall strategy to help church leaders move forward in an entirely different and much more effective way.

In this provocative book, McNeal identifies the six most important realities that church leaders must address including: recapturing the spirit of Christianity and replacing "church growth" with a wider vision of kingdom growth; developing disciples instead of church members; fostering the rise of a new apostolic leadership; focusing on spiritual formation rather than church programs; and shifting from prediction and planning to preparation for the challenges of an uncertain world. McNeal contends that by changing the questions church leaders ask themselves about their congregations and their plans, they can frame the core issues and approach the future with new eyes, new purpose, and new ideas.

Written for congregational leaders, pastors, and staff leaders, _The Present Future_ captures the urgency of a future that is literally now upon us, in a thoughtful, vigorous way. It is filled with examples of leaders and churches who are emerging into a new identity and purpose, and rediscovering the focus of their mission within new spiritual dimensions.

Church Unique

How Missional Leaders Cast Vision, Capture Culture, and Create Movement

Will Mancini

Hardcover
ISBN: 978-0-7879-9679-3

"There is a screaming need today for leaders who will rise above quick fixes and generic approaches. Now, Will Mancini has brought an indispensable book to the church leader's toolbox, providing a thoughtful and creative process that will galvanize your team to unleash God's vision for your church."

—**Howard Hendricks**, chairman, Center for Christian Leadership; distinguished professor, Dallas Theological Seminary

In *Church Unique*, church consultant Will Mancini offers an approach for rethinking what it means to lead with clarity as a visionary. Mancini explains that each church has a culture that reflects its particular values, thoughts, attitudes, and actions, and shows how church leaders can unlock their church's individual DNA and unleash their congregation's one-of-a-kind potential.

Mancini explores the pitfalls churches often fall into in their attempt to grow and explores a new model for vision casting and church growth that has been tested with leaders in all kinds of congregations, including mainline, evangelical, small, and large. The practices and ideas outlined in *Church Unique* will help leaders develop missional teams, articulate unique strategies, unpack the baggage of institutionalism, and live fully into their vision.

Whether leading a megachurch or church plant, a multisite or mainline, a ministry or parachurch, *Church Unique* will provide inspiration as a practical guide for leading into the future. There is a better way.

WILL MANCINI, a former pastor, is the founder of Auxano, a national consulting group that works with traditional and emerging churches and ministries of all types around the country. Their mission is to navigate leaders through growth challenges with vision clarity (www.auxano.com).

The Tangible Kingdom

Creating Incarnational Community

Hugh Halter • Matt Smay

Hardcover
ISBN: 978-0-470-18897-2

"Among increasing numbers of faithful, conservative, Bible-believing Christians, an important shift is beginning to occur. These aren't wild-eyed radicals; they're solid, established church leaders and members who are asking new questions because deep within they discern that something is wrong with the status quo. Hugh and Matt have been through this shift, and offer wise counsel for a way forward."

—**Brian McLaren**, author, *A New Kind of Christian* Trilogy and *Everything Must Change*

Written for those who are trying to nurture authentic faith communities and for those who have struggled to retain their faith, *The Tangible Kingdom* offers theological answers and real-life stories that demonstrate how the best ancient church practices can re-emerge in today's culture, through any church of any size.

The Tangible Kingdom outlines an innovative model for creating thriving grass-roots faith communities, offering new hope for church leaders, pastors, church planters, and churchgoers who are looking for practical new ways to re-orient their lives to fit God's mission today.

HUGH HALTER is a specialist with Church Resource Ministries and the national director of Missio, a global network of missional leaders and church planters. He is also lead architect of Adullam, a congregational network of incarnational communities in Denver, Colorado (www.adullamdenver.com).

MATT SMAY co-directs both Missio and Adullam and specializes in helping existing congregations move toward mission. Halter and Smay direct the MCAP "missional church apprenticeship practicum," an international training network for incarnational church planters, pastors, and emerging leaders (www.missio.us).

Reverse Mentoring

How Young Leaders Can Transform the Church and
Why We Should Let Them

EARL CREPS

Hardcover
ISBN: 978-0-470-18898-9

"The world has ended about four times. New technologies and processes for handling information make the old world obsolete, quickly. When this happens an unusual dynamic asserts itself. Younglings mentor the elders into the way of the new world. The richness of life sharing that is established in reverse mentoring is a largely unexplored, but promising green edge to the Christian movement. Let Earl Creps show you how to get in on this development."
—**Reggie McNeal**, author, _Missional Renaissance_ and _The Present Future_

In this groundbreaking book, Earl Creps addresses how older ministry leaders can learn from younger peers who are in closer touch with today's culture, technology, and social climate. He reveals the practical benefits of reverse mentoring and offers down-to-earth steps for implementing it at both the personal and the organizational level.

Reverse Mentoring offers a guide for leaders who want to experience personal formation by exercising the kind of humility that invites a younger person to become a tutor. Earl Creps details specific benefits of reverse mentoring in areas such as evangelism, communication, and leadership, clearly showing how to develop healthy reverse mentoring relationships that will garner positive results.

Reverse Mentoring is a model for church leaders who understand the importance of learning from younger people to prevent functional obsolescence and to transform their leadership and mission.

EARL CREPS has been a pastor, ministries consultant, and university professor. Along the way, Creps earned a Ph.D. in communication at Northwestern University and a doctor of ministry degree in leadership at AGTS. He is the author of _Off-Road Disciplines_ from Jossey-Bass.